SLOW COOKING RECIPES 2022

SIMPLE AND DELICIOUS RECIPES FOR BEGINNERS

SARINA WILLIAMS

Table of Contents

Pork Chops with Honey and Mustard 11

Smoked Pork with Prunes 13

Sweet Orange Smoked Ham 15

Sherry Chicken with Mashed Potatoes 16

Kicked Up Chicken with Zucchini 18

Festive Cornish Hens 20

Salmon with Caper Sauce 21

Herbed Salmon Loaf with Sauce 23

Lazy Man Mac and Cheese 25

Mediterranean Chicken with Zucchini 26

Mediterranean Stuffed Spaghetti Squash 28

Everyday Tomato Casserole 30

Four Cheese Macaroni Casserole 31

Creamy Vegetable Noodle Casserole 32

Old-Fashioned Pasta Bolognese 34

Mexican Traditional Enchiladas 36

Stuffed Chicken Breasts 38

Pasta with Tomato Sauce 39

Farfalle with Mushroom Sauce	40
Northern Italian Risi Bisi	41
Pecorino and Green Pea Risotto	43
Risotto with Zucchini and Yellow Squash	45
Egg Pie with Mushrooms	47
Aromatic Apple Risotto	49
Delicious Savory Soufflé	50
Spaghetti with Asparagus and Beans	51
Easy Yummy Green Beans	52
Vegan Mediterranean Treat	53
Hot Baked Beans	55
Baked and Herbed Cannellini Beans	57
Delicious Sweet-Spiced Beans	58
Easy Honey Beets with Raisins	60
Glazed Brussels Sprouts with Pearl Onions	61
Herbed Potato-Carrot Purée	62
Winter Cabbage with Bacon	64
Vegetarian Creamed Cabbage	65
Amazing Orange-Glazed Carrots	67
Mediterranean Creamy Cabbage	68
Orange-Glazed Sweet Potatoes	70

Delicious Family Corn Flan 72

Spicy Corn Pudding 73

Pork Shoulder with Hot Sauce 75

Leek and Garlic Custard.. 77

Stuffed Vidalia Onions.. 79

Fruit and Nut Candied Yams 81

Maple Honey Ribs 82

Yam Loaf for Winter Holidays.. 83

Squash and Sweet Potato Pudding 85

Rich and Creamy Potato Gratin 87

Creamy Potatoes with Smoked Ham 89

Creamed Root Vegetables.. 90

Mushroom and Zucchini Soufflé 92

Cheesy Spinach and Noodle Delight 94

Savory Bread Pudding 96

Corn and Potatoes with Shrimp... 98

Rich and Healthy Summer Paella 99

Rabbit in Coconut Sauce 101

Vegetarian Potato and Eggplant Moussaka 102

Curried Chicken Thighs with Potatoes 104

Yummy Evening Pear Clafoutis 106

Evening Risotto with Apples 108

Cheese and Bread Casserole 109

French-Style Sandwiches 111

Bratwurst and Sauerkraut Pitas 112

Romantic Winter Dinner 114

Kicked Up Chicken with Zucchini 115

Festive Cornish Hens 117

Salmon with Caper Sauce 118

Cheesy Monkfish Chowder with Cauliflower 120

Hearty Flounder Chowder 122

Rich Seafood Soup with Bacon 124

Refreshing Fish Chowder with Eggs 126

Spicy Sweet Potato Chili 128

Chili with Turkey and Roasted Pepper 130

Black Bean Chili with Squash 132

Turkey and Cannellini Bean Chili 134

Easy Beef and Pork Chili 136

Italian-Style Chili 138

Family Favourite Chili 140

Easy Tenderloin Chili 142

Yummy Tomato Bean Soup 143

Lamb Chili with Ham 145

Creamy Vegetable Soup 147

Fall Brussels sprouts Soup 148

Vegetarian Creamed Corn Soup 150

Rich Potato Pistou Soup 152

Refreshing Roasted Red Pepper Soup 154

Old-Fashioned Beef Stew 156

Tangy Cucumber Soup 158

Easy Yummy Beef Stew 160

Hearty Chicken Stew 162

Sausage and Turkey Stew 164

Turkey and Kidney Bean Stew 165

Cod and Shrimp Stew 167

Summer Spiced Fish Stew 169

Vegetarian Stew for All Seasons 171

Vegan Wheat Berry and Lentil Stew 173

Family Red Chili 174

Turkey Chili with Kale 176

Piquant Chicken Sausage Chili 178

Pepperoni Hot Chili 180

Spaghetti with Beans and Asparagus 182

- Easy Spicy Green Beans 184
- Favorite Creamy Green Beans 186
- Steak Roll Ups with Mushrooms 187
- Favorite Hot Rouladen 189
- Juicy Beef Short Ribs 191
- Easy Italian-Style Meatloaf 192
- Cheesy Everyday Meatloaf 194
- Curried Peanut Meat Loaf 196
- Mom's Spiced Mashed Beans 198
- Kicked Up Cajun Jambalaya 199
- Tangy Pork Roast 201
- Hearty Stuffed Cabbage Leaves 203
- Milk Braised Pork Loin 205
- Mashed Potatoes with Carrots 207
- Holiday Cooked Ham 209
- Family Favourite Apple Butter 210
- Italian-style Chicken with Broccoli 211
- Herbed Salmon Loaf with Sauce 213
- Lazy Man Mac and Cheese 215
- Mediterranean Chicken with Zucchini 216
- Mediterranean Stuffed Spaghetti Squash 218

Pork Chops with Honey and Mustard

(Ready in about 4 hours | Servings 4)

Ingredients

- 4 loin pork chops, boneless
- 1/4 cup leeks, chopped
- 1/2 cup chicken broth
- 1/2 cup dry white wine
- 1 tablespoon cornstarch
- 2 tablespoons honey
- 2 tablespoons mustard
- 1 teaspoon grated ginger
- Salt, to taste
- Black pepper, to taste

Directions

1. Combine pork chops, leeks, chicken broth and white wine in a crock pot.

2. Cover and cook on low about 3 to 4 hours.

3. Remove pork chops from the crock pot and keep warm.

4. Add cornstarch, honey, mustard, ginger, salt and black pepper; continue cooking about 5 minutes. Serve warm.

Smoked Pork with Prunes

(Ready in about 8 hours | Servings 8)

Ingredients

- 2 pounds pork loin, boneless and cubed
- 1 cup prunes, pitted
- 1 ½ cups vegetable broth
- 1/2 cup dry white wine
- 1 teaspoon lemon juice
- Salt, to taste
- Black pepper, to taste
- Smoked paprika, to taste
- 2 tablespoons corn starch
- 1/4 cup cold water
- Liquid smoke, to taste
- 4 cups cooked couscous, warm

Directions

1. Place all of the ingredients, except corn starch, water, liquid smoke and couscous, in a crock pot.

2. Cover and cook on low approximately 8 hours. Next, turn heat to high; cook about 10 minutes.

3. In a bowl, combine corn starch with cold water. Add this mixture and liquid smoke to the crock pot and stir constantly 2 to 3 minutes. Serve with couscous.

Sweet Orange Smoked Ham

(Ready in about 3 hours | Servings 10)

Ingredients

- 3 pounds smoked ham, boneless
- 1/3 cup orange juice
- 1/4 cup honey
- 1 teaspoon allspice
- 1/2 teaspoon ground cinnamon
- 11/2 tablespoons corn starch
- 1/4 cup cold water
- 2 tablespoons dry sherry

Directions

1. Put all of the ingredients, except corn starch, water and sherry, into a crock pot.

2. Cover and cook on low until ham is tender or about 3 hours. Transfer prepared ham to a serving platter.

3. Measure 1 cup broth into skillet; heat to boiling; whisk in combined remaining ingredients about 1 minute.

4. Serve ham with sauce and enjoy!

Sherry Chicken with Mashed Potatoes

(Ready in about 4 hours | Servings 4)

Ingredients

For the Sherry Chicken:
- 1/4 cup dry sherry
- 1 cup raisins
- 4 medium-sized chicken breast
- 1 tart cooking apple, peeled and chopped
- 1 sweet onion, sliced
- 1 cup chicken broth
- Salt and pepper, to taste

For the mashed Potatoes:
- 2 pounds Idaho potatoes, peeled and cooked
- 1/4 sour cream
- 1/3 cup whole milk
- 2 tablespoons butter
- 1 teaspoon sea salt
- 1/4 teaspoon black pepper
- 1/4 teaspoon cayenne pepper

Directions

1. In a crock pot, place all of the ingredients for the sherry chicken; cover and cook on high until chicken breasts are tender or 3 to 4 hours.

2. Meanwhile, beat potatoes, adding sour cream, milk, and butter; beat until smooth and uniform.

3. Season with spices and serve on the side with sherry chicken.

Kicked Up Chicken with Zucchini

(Ready in about 4 hours | Servings 6)

Ingredients

- 3 medium-sized chicken breasts, halved
- 1 cup almond milk
- 1/4 cup water
- 1/4 cup lemon juice
- 2 cloves garlic, minced
- 1 medium-sized onion, chopped
- Salt, to taste
- Red pepper, to taste
- 1 teaspoon ground ginger
- 1 teaspoon ground cumin
- 1 pound zucchini, sliced
- 1 tablespoon cornflour
- 2 tablespoons water
- 1/3 cup fresh parsley, chopped
- 4 cups rice, cooked

Directions

1. Place all ingredients, except zucchini, cornflour, water, parsley and rice, in your crock pot.

2. Cover and cook on low heat setting about 4 hours, adding zucchini during last 30 minutes of cooking time. Reserve chicken breasts.

3. Turn heat to high and continue cooking 10 minutes; stir in combined cornflour and water, stirring about 3 minutes.

4. Sprinkle with parsley; serve over rice.

Festive Cornish Hens

(Ready in about 6 hours | Servings 4)

Ingredients

- 2 frozen Cornish hens, thawed
- 1/2 teaspoon sea salt
- 1/4 teaspoon ground black pepper
- 1/2 teaspoon cayenne pepper
- 1 clove garlic, minced
- 1/3 cup chicken broth
- 2 tablespoons cornflour
- 1/4 cup water

Directions

1. Sprinkle Cornish hens with salt, black pepper and cayenne pepper; add minced garlic and place in a crock pot. Pour in chicken broth.
2. Cover and cook on low 6 hours. Remove Cornish hens and reserve.
3. Stir in combined cornflour and water, stirring 2 to 3 minutes; serve.

Salmon with Caper Sauce

(Ready in about 45 minutes | Servings 4)

Ingredients

- 1/2 cup dry white wine
- 1/2 cup water
- 1 yellow onion, thin sliced
- 1/2 teaspoon salt
- 1/4 teaspoon black pepper
- 4 salmon steaks
- 2 tablespoons butter
- 3 tablespoons flour
- 1 cup chicken broth
- 2 teaspoons lemon juice
- 3 tablespoons capers

Directions

1. Combine wine, water, onion, salt and black pepper in a crock pot; cover and cook on high 20 minutes.

2. Add salmon steaks; cover and cook on high until salmon is tender or about 20 minutes.

3. To make the sauce, in a small skillet, melt butter over medium flame. Stir in flour and cook for 1 minute.

4. Pour in chicken broth and lemon juice; whisk for 1 to 2 minutes. Add capers; serve the sauce with salmon.

Herbed Salmon Loaf with Sauce

(Ready in about 5 hours | Servings 4)

Ingredients

For the Salmon Meatloaf:
- 1 cup fresh bread crumbs
- 1 can (7 ½ ounce) salmon, drained
- 1/4 cup scallions, chopped
- 1/3 cup whole milk
- 1 egg
- 1 tablespoon fresh lemon juice
- 1 teaspoon dried rosemary
- 1 teaspoon ground coriander
- 1/2 teaspoon fenugreek
- 1 teaspoon mustard seed
- 1/2 teaspoon salt
- 1/4 teaspoon white pepper

For the Sauce:
- 1/2 cup cucumber, chopped
- 1/2 cup reduced-fat plain yogurt
- 1/2 teaspoon dill weed

- Salt, to taste

Directions

1. Line your crock pot with a foil.

2. Mix all ingredients for the salmon meatloaf until everything is well incorporated; form into loaf and place in the crock pot.

3. Cover with a suitable lid and cook on low heat setting 5 hours.

4. Combine all of the ingredients for the sauce; whisk to combine.

5. Serve your meatloaf with prepared sauce.

Lazy Man Mac and Cheese

(Ready in about 4 hours | Servings 4)

Ingredients

- Non-stick cooking spray-butter flavour
- 16 ounces macaroni of choice
- 1/2 cup butter, melted
- 1 (12-ounce) can evaporated milk
- 1 cup milk
- 4 cups Colby jack cheese, grated

Directions

1. Lightly grease a crock pot with cooking spray.

2. First of all, cook your favourite macaroni according to package directions; rinse and drain; transfer to the crock pot.

3. Add the rest of ingredients and stir well. Cook on low heat setting 3 to 4 hours. Enjoy!

Mediterranean Chicken with Zucchini

(Ready in about 8 hours | Servings 4)

Ingredients

- 4 medium-sized chicken breasts, skinless
- 2 cups petite-diced tomatoes
- 1 stock cube
- 1/2 cup dry white wine
- 1/2 cup water
- 1 medium zucchini, sliced
- 1 large-sized onion, chopped
- 1/3 cup fennel bulb, chopped
- 1 teaspoon ground cumin
- 1 teaspoon dried basil leaves
- 1 bay leaf
- A pinch of black pepper
- 1/4 cup olives, pitted and sliced
- 1 teaspoon lemon juice
- 3 cups cooked rice

Directions

1. Place all ingredients, except olives, lemon juice and cooked rice, in a crock pot; cover and cook on low about 8 hours, adding pitted olives during last 30 minutes of cooking time.

2. Add lemon juice; discard bay leaf. Serve over cooked rice and enjoy.

Mediterranean Stuffed Spaghetti Squash

(Ready in about 8 hours | Servings 4)

Ingredients

- 1 medium-sized spaghetti squash, halved lengthwise and seeded
- 2 Roma tomatoes, diced
- 2 cans (6-ounces) tuna in water, drained and flaked
- 1 teaspoon dried basil leaves
- 1 teaspoon dried oregano leaves
- 1/2 teaspoon dried thyme
- Salt, to taste
- Black pepper, to taste
- Cayenne pepper, to taste
- 1/2 cup water
- 1/4 cup Pecorino Romano, grated

Directions

1. Place squash halves on a plate.

2. In a measuring cup or a mixing bowl, combine all of the ingredients, except water and Pecorino Romano. Spoon this mixture into squash halves and place in the crock pot.

3. Add water to the crock pot; cover and cook 6 to 8 hours on low.

4. Sprinkle with Pecorino Romano and serve.

Everyday Tomato Casserole

(Ready in about 3 hours | Servings 6)

Ingredients

- 8 ounces macaroni, cooked
- 1 can (16-ounce) petite-diced tomatoes, drained
- 1/2 cup leeks, chopped
- 1 cup whole milk
- 1 cup water
- 1 tablespoon cornflour
- 3 eggs, lightly beaten
- 1/2 cup sharp cheese, grated
- 1/2 teaspoon ground cinnamon
- Salt, to taste
- Paprika, as garnish

Directions

1. Combine macaroni, tomatoes and leeks in a crock pot.

2. In a bowl, mix remaining ingredients, except paprika; pour over macaroni in the crock pot.

3. Cook on low about 3 hours or until custard is set; divide among serving plates and sprinkle with paprika.

Four Cheese Macaroni Casserole

(Ready in about 3 hours | Servings 8)

Ingredients

- Non-stick cooking spray-butter flavour
- 3 cups whole milk
- 1/3 cup all-purpose flour
- 1 cup Colby-Jack, crumbled
- 1 cup reduced-fat mozzarella, shredded
- 1 cup Cheddar cheese, shredded
- 1 pound macaroni, cooked al dente
- 1/2 cup Parmesan cheese

Directions

1. Treat a crock pot with cooking spray.
2. In a large mixing bowl, combine milk and flour until smooth; add the rest of ingredients, except macaroni and Parmesan cheese.
3. Stir in macaroni and sprinkle with Parmesan cheese.
4. Cover and cook on low 3 hours.

Creamy Vegetable Noodle Casserole

(Ready in about 5 hours | Servings 6)

Ingredients

- 1 cup 2% reduced-fat milk
- 1 ½ cups cream of mushroom soup
- 2 tablespoons mayonnaise, reduced-fat
- 1 cup processed cheese, shredded
- 1 green bell pepper
- 1 large-sized carrot, chopped
- 1/3 celery stalk, chopped
- 1/3 cup onion, chopped
- 1/4 teaspoon sea salt
- 1/4 teaspoon ground black pepper
- 6 ounces noodles, cooked al dente
- 1/2 cup chickpea
- 1 tablespoon butter
- 1/3 cup fresh bread crumbs
- 1/3 cup pine nuts, chopped

Directions

1. In a crock pot, combine first ten ingredients.

2. Stir in cooked noodles; cover with a suitable lid and cook on low 5 hours. Add chickpeas during last 30 minutes of cooking time.

3. In a cast-iron skillet, melt butter over medium heat; cook bread crumbs and pine nuts about 5 minutes. Sprinkle on prepared casserole and serve!

Old-Fashioned Pasta Bolognese

(Ready in about 7 hours | Servings 6)

Ingredients

- 1/2 pound ground pork
- 1/2 pound ground beef
- 1/4 cup onion, chopped
- 3 cloves garlic, minced
- 1/4 cup carrot, chopped
- 1 1/2 teaspoons dried Italian seasoning
- 1 can (8-ounces) tomato sauce, undrained,
- 1 large-sized tomato, diced
- 1/4 cup dry red wine
- 1 teaspoon sea salt
- 1/4 teaspoon pepper
- 1/4 teaspoon cayenne pepper
- 12 ounces spaghetti, cooked

Directions

1. In a non-stick heavy skillet, brown ground meat over medium heat for 8 minutes; crumble with a fork.

2. Add remaining ingredients, except spaghetti, to the crock pot. Cover and cook on low 6 to 7 hours.

3. Ladle prepared sauce over spaghetti and serve warm.

Mexican Traditional Enchiladas

(Ready in about 1 hour 15 minutes | Servings 6)

Ingredients

- 1 pound mixed ground beef and pork
- 3 slices of Canadian bacon, chopped
- 1 ¼ cups water
- 1 (1-ounce) package taco seasoning mix
- 1 cup chunky salsa
- 2 cups chicken stock
- Sea salt, to taste
- 4 cups Mexican cheese blend, shredded
- 10 corn tortillas, quartered

Directions

1. In a wide saucepan, cook ground meat and bacon over medium heat. Cook until they are browned or about 10 minutes.

2. In a medium-sized mixing bowl, combine together water, taco seasoning mix, salsa, chicken stock, salt and 2 cups of cheese.

3. Arrange a layer of tortillas on the bottom of a crock pot. Add a layer of the ground beef, and then spoon a layer of the salsa mixture over that.

4. Repeat the layers one more time, ending with the layer of tortillas. Top with remaining 2 cups of cheese.

5. Cover with a lid; cook on high for 1 hour.

Stuffed Chicken Breasts

(Ready in about 3 hours | Servings 4)

Ingredients

- 1/2 cup sharp cheese, shredded
- 1 red bell pepper, chopped
- 1 green bell pepper, chopped
- 1 yellow bell pepper, chopped
- 2 heaping tablespoons fresh parsley, chopped
- 1/4 cup cilantro, minced
- 1/4 cup tomatoes, diced
- 1/2 teaspoon chili powder
- 1/2 teaspoon celery salt
- 4 small-sized chicken breast, boneless and pounded to 1/4 inch thickness

Directions

1. In a bowl, mix together all of the ingredients, except chicken.

2. Spread this mixture on the chicken breast. Roll up chicken breasts tightly and secure them with toothpicks or the skewers.

3. Arrange the chicken rolls in the crock pot. Cover and cook 3 hours on high.

Pasta with Tomato Sauce

(Ready in about 7 hours | Servings 6)

Ingredients

- 4 large-sized tomatoes, chopped
- 1 large-sized yellow onion, finely chopped
- 2 cloves garlic, minced
- 1/2 cup dry red wine
- 2 tablespoons tomato ketchup
- 1 tablespoon brown sugar
- 1 teaspoon dried oregano leaves
- 1 teaspoon celery seeds
- 1 teaspoon dried thyme leaves
- 1/8 teaspoon paprika
- 1/4 teaspoon kosher salt
- 12 ounces pasta, cooked and warm

Directions

1. Combine all of the ingredients, except pasta, in your crock pot.
2. Cover and cook 7 hours on low.
3. Ladle sauce over pasta and enjoy.

Farfalle with Mushroom Sauce

(Ready in about 8 hours | Servings 6)

Ingredients

- 1 onion, finely chopped
- 2 cloves garlic, minced
- 1 medium-sized plum tomatoes, chopped
- 1 ½ cups cream of mushroom soup
- 2 tablespoons tomato ketchup
- 1 tablespoon brown sugar
- 1 teaspoon dried oregano leaves
- 1 cup mushrooms, thinly sliced
- 1 teaspoon dried basil leaves
- 1/4 teaspoon kosher salt
- 1/4 teaspoon ground black pepper
- 12 ounces Farfalle, cooked and warm

Directions

1. In a crock pot, place all ingredients, except farfalle.
2. Cover with a lid and cook about 8 hours on low.
3. Ladle mushroom sauce over Farfalle and serve.

Northern Italian Risi Bisi

(Ready in about 1 hour 30 minutes | Servings 4)

Ingredients

- 1 cup water
- 2 cups vegetable stock
- 1/2 cup green onions, finely chopped
- 2 cloves garlic, minced
- 1 ½ cups rice
- 1 teaspoon dried oregano leaves
- 1 tablespoon dried basil leaves
- Ground black pepper, to taste
- Cayenne pepper, to taste
- 8 ounces green peas, trimmed
- 1 teaspoon fresh lemon juice
- 1/2 cup Parmesan cheese, grated

Directions

1. In a crock pot, arrange all ingredients, except green peas, lemon juice and cheese.

2. Cover and cook on high heat setting about 1 ¼ hours or until the liquid is almost absorbed. Add green peas in the last 15 minutes of cooking time.

3. Stir in lemon juice and cheese; divide among serving plates and serve.

Pecorino and Green Pea Risotto

(Ready in about 1 hour 30 minutes | Servings 4)

Ingredients

- 2 cups vegetable stock
- 1 cup tomato juice
- 1/2 cup shallots, finely chopped
- 2 cloves garlic, minced
- 1 ½ cups cooked chicken, cubed
- 1 ½ cups rice
- 1 teaspoon dried Italian seasoning
- Salt, to taste
- Ground black pepper, to taste
- Paprika, to taste
- 8 ounces green peas, trimmed
- 1/2 cup Pecorino cheese, grated

Directions

1. In your crock pot, place all ingredients, except green peas and Pecorino cheese.

2. Cover; cook on high about 1 hour 30 minutes, adding green peas during last 15 minutes of cooking time.

3. Add cheese and serve warm.

Risotto with Zucchini and Yellow Squash

(Ready in about 1 hour 25 minutes | Servings 4)

Ingredients

- 3 cups vegetable broth
- 1 medium-sized onion, chopped
- 2 cloves garlic, minced
- 1 cup sliced cremini mushrooms
- 1 teaspoon dried rosemary
- 1 ½ cups short-grain rice
- 1 cup each zucchini, cubed
- 3/4 cup summer yellow squash, cubed
- 1 sweet potato, peeled cubed
- 1/4 cup Pecorino cheese, grated
- 1/2 teaspoon sea salt
- 1/2 teaspoon ground black pepper
- 1/2 teaspoon cayenne pepper

Directions

1. Combine all ingredients, except cheese, in your crock pot.

2. Cover and cook on high about 1 ¼ hours or until rice is al dente.

3. Stir in cheese; divide among four serving plates and enjoy.

Egg Pie with Mushrooms

(Ready in about 4 hours | Servings 4)

Ingredients

- 4 large-sized eggs
- 1/4 cup all-purpose flour
- 1/2 teaspoon baking soda
- 1/4 teaspoon salt
- 1/8 teaspoon freshly ground black pepper
- 2 cups Colby Jack cheese, shredded
- 1 cup reduced-fat cottage cheese
- 1 Chipotle pepper, minced
- 1 cup mushrooms, sliced
- 1/2 teaspoon dried rosemary
- 1/2 teaspoon dried basil leaves

Directions

1. In a large bowl, beat the eggs until foamy; mix in flour, baking soda, salt, and ground black pepper. Stir in remaining ingredients.

2. Pour the mixture into oiled crock pot; cover and cook about 4 hours on low.

3. Divide among four serving plates and enjoy!

Aromatic Apple Risotto

(Ready in about 9 hours | Servings 6)

Ingredients

- 1/4 cup butter, melted
- 1 ½ cups Arborio rice
- 3 apples, cored and sliced
- 1/4 teaspoon freshly ground nutmeg
- 1/4 teaspoon ground cloves
- 1 teaspoon ground cinnamon
- 1/3 cup brown sugar
- A pinch of salt
- 1 cup apple juice
- 2 cups whole milk
- 1 cup water

Directions

1. Add the butter and rice to the crock pot.
2. Then, add the rest of ingredients; stir to combine.
3. Cover and cook 9 hours on low. Serve with dried fruit, if desired.

Delicious Savory Soufflé

(Ready in about 3 hours | Servings 8)

Ingredients
- 8 slices of bread
- 8 ounces Cheddar cheese, shredded
- 8 ounces mozzarella cheese, shredded
- Non-stick cooking spray
- 2 cups fat-free evaporated milk
- 4 eggs
- 1/4 teaspoon allspice

Directions

1. Tear the bread into pieces and reserve.

2. Combine the cheeses and reserve.

3. Grease your crock pot with non-stick cooking spray. Then, add bread and cheese. Stir to combine.

4. In a measuring cup or a mixing bowl, whisk the milk, eggs, and allspice. Pour over the bread and cheese in the crock pot. Cook 2 to 3 hours on low.

5. Serve sprinkled with pitted and chopped olives, if desired.

Spaghetti with Asparagus and Beans

(Ready in about 3 hours | Servings 8)

Ingredients

- 1 can (15-ounce) Great Northern beans, rinsed and drained
- 3/4 cup vegetable stock
- 2 tomatoes, chopped plum
- 1 carrot, chopped
- 1 teaspoon dried basil leaves
- 1 teaspoon dried rosemary leaves
- Salt and pepper, to taste
- 1 pound asparagus, sliced
- 8 ounces spaghetti, cooked
- 1/2 cup Parmesan cheese, shredded

Directions

1. Combine all ingredients, except asparagus, spaghetti and cheese, in your crock pot.

2. Cook on low about 3 hours, adding asparagus during last 30 minutes of cooking time.

3. Adjust seasonings to your taste, then, add spaghetti and Parmesan cheese; serve.

Easy Yummy Green Beans

(Ready in about 4 hours | Servings 8)

Ingredients

- 1 pound green beans
- 4 large-sized tomatoes, chopped
- 1/2 cup shallots, chopped
- 3 cloves garlic, minced
- 1 teaspoon dried basil leaves
- 1 teaspoon dried rosemary
- 1/2 teaspoon celery salt
- 1/4 teaspoon black pepper
- 1/4 teaspoon cayenne pepper

Directions

1. Combine all ingredients in your crock pot.
2. Cover with a lid; then, cook on high about 4 hours or until beans are tender.
3. Serve with poultry entrée.

Vegan Mediterranean Treat

(Ready in about 2 hours | Servings 8)

Ingredients

- 2 cups green beans
- 1/4 cup onion, finely chopped
- 2 cloves garlic, minced
- 1 large-sized red bell pepper, chopped
- 1 large-sized carrot, chopped
- 1 teaspoon ginger root, ground
- 1/2 cup water
- 1 cup canned black beans, drained
- 1 tablespoon rice wine vinegar
- 2 teaspoons tamari sauce
- 1/2 teaspoon sea salt
- 1/4 teaspoon ground black pepper

Directions

1. In your crock pot, combine green beans, onion, garlic, bell pepper, carrot, ginger root, and water; cover with a lid and set the crock pot to high.

2. Cook about 1 ½ hours; drain. Add remaining ingredients and cook 30 minutes longer. Taste, adjust the seasonings and serve.

Hot Baked Beans

(Ready in about 6 hours | Servings 8)

Ingredients

- 1 cup chopped onion
- 2 cans (15-ounce) pinto beans, rinsed and drained
- 1 serrano pepper, chopped
- 1 jalapeño chili, finely chopped
- 1 cup whole kernel corn
- 1 cup cherry tomatoes, halved
- 2 tablespoons sugar
- 1/2 teaspoon dried thyme leaves
- 1 bay leaf
- 1/2 teaspoon sea salt
- 1/4 teaspoon white pepper
- 1/2 cup Pecorino cheese, grated
- 1/4 cup fresh parsley, finely chopped

Directions

1. Combine all ingredients, except cheese and parsley, in your crock pot.

2. Cover and cook on low 5 to 6 hours.

3. Sprinkle with cheese and parsley and serve!

Baked and Herbed Cannellini Beans

(Ready in about 6 hours | Servings 6)

Ingredients

- 1 cup vegetable broth
- 3 cans (15-ounces) cannellini beans
- 1/2 cup leeks, chopped
- 2-3 cloves garlic, minced
- 1 celery stalk, chopped
- 1 sweet red bell pepper, chopped
- 1 teaspoon dried sage
- 2 bay leaves
- 6 sun-dried tomatoes, softened and sliced
- 1/2 teaspoon paprika
- 1/2 teaspoon sea salt
- 1/4 teaspoon freshly ground black pepper

Directions

1. Put all of the ingredients into your crock pot.
2. Cover and cook 5 to 6 hours on low. Serve with sausage and your favorite salad, if desired.

Delicious Sweet-Spiced Beans

(Ready in about 6 hours | Servings 10)

Ingredients

- 1 ½ cups leeks, chopped
- 4 cans (15-ounce) Great Northern beans, rinsed and drained
- 2 tablespoons gingerroot, finely chopped
- 3 cloves garlic, minced
- 1 tablespoon sugar
- 1 cup tomato paste
- 1 teaspoon mustard seeds
- 1 teaspoon dried thyme leaves
- 1 teaspoon dried sage leaves
- 1/4 teaspoon nutmeg, grated
- 2 bay leaves
- Black pepper, to taste
- 5-6 peppercorns
- 1/2 cup gingersnap crumbs, coarsely ground

Directions

1. Combine all ingredients, except gingersnap crumbs, in a crock pot.

2. Cover the crock pot with a lid and cook 6 hours on low, adding gingersnap crumbs during last hour.

3. Discard bay leaves and serve warm.

Easy Honey Beets with Raisins

(Ready in about 2 hours 30 minutes | Servings 6)

Ingredients

- 2 cups hot water
- 1 ½ pounds medium beets
- 1 large-sized red onion, finely chopped
- 2 cloves garlic, minced
- 1/4 cup raisins
- 3 heaping tablespoons pine nuts, toasted
- 1/4 cup honey
- 3 tablespoons red wine vinegar
- 1 tablespoon olive oil
- Salt and pepper, to taste

Directions

1. In a crock pot, place hot water and beets; cover and cook on high approximately 2 hours; drain.

2. Next, peel beets and cut into small pieces. Return to the crock pot; add remaining ingredients.

3. Cook for 30 minutes longer. Serve with poultry entrée and enjoy!

Glazed Brussels Sprouts with Pearl Onions

(Ready in about 2 hours 10 minutes | Servings 6)

Ingredients

- 8 ounces frozen pearl onions, thawed
- 8 ounces small Brussels sprouts
- 1 1/2 cups hot water
- 1/4 teaspoon ground black pepper
- 1/4 teaspoon cayenne pepper
- 1/2 teaspoon sea salt
- 1 tablespoon margarine
- 1/4 cup brown sugar

Directions

1. Combine pearl onions, Brussels sprouts and hot water in a crock pot.

2. Cover with a lid and cook on high about 2 hours or until the vegetables are tender; drain. Season with black pepper, cayenne pepper, and sea salt.

3. Add margarine and sugar and cook 10 more minutes. Serve warm and enjoy.

Herbed Potato-Carrot Purée

(Ready in about 3 hours 30 minutes | Servings 8)

Ingredients

- 2 cups potato, peeled cubed
- 2 pounds carrots, sliced
- 1 cup water
- 2 tablespoons butter
- 1/4 cup milk, warm
- 1/2 teaspoon dried rosemary
- 1/2 teaspoon allspice
- 1/2 teaspoon celery seeds
- 1 teaspoon dried basil
- 1 teaspoon dried oregano
- 1/2 teaspoon salt
- 1/2 teaspoon red pepper flakes, crushed

Directions

1. Place potatoes, carrots and water in your crock pot; cover with a lid and cook 3 hours on high. Drain well.

2. Purée cooked potato and carrots in a food processor until creamy and uniform; return to the crock pot. Uncover and cook on high about 30 minutes; stir occasionally.

3. Beat butter and milk into mashed potatoes and carrots. Make a creamy consistency. Season with spices and serve.

Winter Cabbage with Bacon

(Ready in about 4 hours | Servings 6)

Ingredients
- 1 head cabbage, thinly sliced
- 3/4 cup leeks, chopped
- 2 medium-sized carrots, chopped
- 1 sweet red bell pepper, thinly sliced
- 2 cloves garlic, minced
- 1/2 teaspoon anise seeds
- 1/4 cup canned beef broth
- 1/4 cup dry white wine
- Salt, to taste
- 1/2 teaspoon ground black pepper
- 2 slices of diced bacon, cooked crisp and drained

Directions
1. Combine all ingredients, except bacon, in your crock pot.
2. Cover and cook on high about 4 hours or until cabbage is tender.
3. Add bacon, adjust the seasonings to taste, and enjoy!

Vegetarian Creamed Cabbage

(Ready in about 4 hours 10 minutes | Servings 6)

Ingredients

- 1 large-sized head cabbage, thinly sliced
- 3/4 cup red or yellow onion, chopped
- 2 medium-sized carrots, chopped
- 1 sweet bell pepper, thinly sliced
- 2 cloves garlic, minced
- 1/2 teaspoon caraway seeds
- 1/2 teaspoon celery seeds
- 1 cup canned vegetable stock
- Salt, to taste
- Ground black pepper, to taste
- Cayenne pepper, to taste
- 1/2 cup reduced-fat sour cream
- 1 tablespoon cornflour

Directions

1. In your crock pot, place all ingredients, except sour cream and cornflour.

2. Cover with a lid and cook 4 hours on high.

3. Stir in combined sour cream and cornflour and continue cooking 10 minutes longer. Serve warm.

Amazing Orange-Glazed Carrots

(Ready in about 3 hours 10 minutes | Servings 4)

Ingredients

- 1 pound baby carrots
- 3/4 cup orange juice
- 1 tablespoon butter
- 1/2 cup brown sugar, packed light
- 1/2 teaspoon allspice
- 1/4 teaspoon ground mace
- 1/2 teaspoon sea salt
- 1/2 teaspoon white pepper
- 2 tablespoons cornflour
- 1/4 cup water

Directions

1. In a crock pot, place all ingredients, except cornflour and water; cover and cook on high about 3 hours or until carrots are crisp-tender.

2. In a small mixing bowl, combine cornflour and water; add to the crock pot. Stir 2 to 3 minutes.

3. Divide among four serving plates and serve with meat or fish entrée, if desired.

Mediterranean Creamy Cabbage

(Ready in about 4 hours 10 minutes | Servings 6)

Ingredients

- 1 large-sized head Savoy cabbage, sliced
- 3/4 cup red or yellow onion, chopped
- 1 celery rib, chopped
- 1 green bell pepper, thinly sliced
- 1 yellow bell pepper, thinly sliced
- 2 cloves garlic, minced
- 1 teaspoon celery seeds
- 1 cup canned vegetable stock
- Salt, to taste
- Ground black pepper, to taste
- Paprika, to taste
- Grating of nutmeg
- 1 cup spinach, torn into pieces
- 1/2 cup plain Greek yogurt
- 1 tablespoon corn starch

Directions

1. In a crock pot, arrange all of the ingredients, except spinach, yogurt and corn starch.

2. Cook covered for 4 hours, adding the spinach during last 30 minutes of cooking time and sprinkling with some extra spices, if desired.

3. Add combined yogurt and corn starch, stirring about 10 minutes. Serve warm and enjoy!

Orange-Glazed Sweet Potatoes

(Ready in about 3 hours 5 minutes | Servings 4)

Ingredients

- 1 pound sweet potatoes
- 3/4 cup orange juice
- 1 tablespoon margarine
- 1/2 cup brown sugar
- 1/2 teaspoon grated nutmeg
- 1/4 teaspoon ground mace
- 1/4 teaspoon ground cloves
- 1/2 teaspoon ground cinnamon
- 1/2 teaspoon kosher salt
- 1/2 teaspoon white pepper
- 2 tablespoons cornflour
- 1/4 cup water

Directions

1. Place all ingredients, except cornflour and water, in a crock pot.

2. Cover and cook on high about 3 hours or until sweet potatoes are crisp-tender.

3. Add combined cornflour and water, stirring constantly 3 to 4 minutes. Serve with your favorite meat entrée.

Delicious Family Corn Flan

(Ready in about 3 hours | Servings 6)

Ingredients

- 1 teaspoon sugar
- 1 cup milk
- 3 eggs, lightly beaten
- 1 ½ cup creamed corn
- 1 cup kernel corn
- 1/2 teaspoon allspice
- 1/2 teaspoon salt
- 1/4 teaspoon white pepper

Directions

1. Mix all of the ingredients together. Place in a soufflé dish.
2. Place this soufflé dish on a rack in the crock pot.
3. Cover and cook on low about 3 hours.

Spicy Corn Pudding

(Ready in about 3 hours | Servings 6)

Ingredients

- Non-stick cooking spray
- 3 medium-sized eggs
- 1 cup whole milk
- 1/2 cup frozen whole kernel corn, thawed
- 2 tablespoons all-purpose flour
- 1/2 teaspoon ground cumin
- 1 teaspoon fine sea salt
- 1/4 teaspoon red pepper flakes, crushed
- 1/4 teaspoon black pepper
- 1/2 cup creamed corn
- 2 cups reduced-fat sharp cheese, shredded
- 1 chipotle pepper, minced

Directions

1. Treat the inside of your crock pot with non-stick cooking spray.

2. Purée eggs, milk, whole-kernel corn, all-purpose flour, cumin, salt, red pepper flakes and black pepper in your food processor or a blender until uniform and smooth.

3. Pour the mixture into the oiled crock pot. Add the rest of the ingredients.

4. Cover and cook about 3 hours on low.

Pork Shoulder with Hot Sauce

(Ready in about 12 hours | Servings 10)

Ingredients

- 1 pork shoulder roast
- 1/2 teaspoon ground black pepper
- 1/2 teaspoon cayenne pepper
- 1 teaspoon fine sea salt
- 1 tablespoon fresh orange juice
- 1 cup balsamic vinegar
- 2 tablespoons brown sugar
- 1 tablespoon Tabasco sauce

Directions

1. On the bottom of your crock pot, place the pork. Season with black pepper, cayenne pepper, and sea salt. Pour in orange juice and balsamic vinegar.

2. Cover and cook 12 hours on low.

3. Remove the pork from the crock pot; discard any bones.

4. To make the sauce, save 2 cups of liquid. Add sugar and tabasco sauce to the reserved liquid.

5. Shred the pork and return to the crock pot. Pour the sauce over the pork.

6. Keep warm before serving time.

Leek and Garlic Custard

(Ready in about 3 hours | Servings 6)

Ingredients

- 2 tablespoons extra-virgin olive oil
- 4 leeks (white parts only), sliced
- 2 cloves garlic, minced
- 1/2 teaspoon allspice
- 2 eggs, lightly beaten
- 1 cup whole milk
- 1/8 teaspoon ground nutmeg
- 1/2 teaspoon sea salt
- 1/4 teaspoon ground black pepper
- 1/4 teaspoon red pepper flakes, crushed
- 1/2 cup Swiss cheese, shredded

Directions

1. In a small cast-iron skillet, heat olive oil over medium-high. Sauté leeks and garlic about 8 minutes.

2. Add sautéed leeks and garlic to a suitable soufflé dish; add remaining ingredients; place on a rack in your crock pot.

3. Cover and cook on low 3 to 3 ½ hours or until custard is set.

4. Let stand for 10 minutes before slicing and serving. This custard can be a delicious dinner and it also will complement your favorite entrée.

Stuffed Vidalia Onions

(Ready in about 4 hours | Servings 6)

Ingredients

- 4 medium-sized Vidalia onions, peeled
- 1/2 cup bread crumbs
- 1/2 cup Queso fresco cheese, Crumbled
- 4 sun-dried tomatoes, chopped
- 1/4 cup water chestnut
- 2 cloves garlic, minced
- 1/2 teaspoon dried basil leaves
- 1/4 teaspoon salt
- 1/4 teaspoon black pepper
- 1 egg white
- 1/2 cup warm chicken stock

Directions

1. Boil Vidalia onions in water about 10 minutes; drain.

2. Cut Vidalia onions into halves and remove centres. You can reserve centres for another use.

3. In a mixing bowl, mix together remaining ingredients, except chicken stock; fill onion halves with prepared mixture.

4. Add stuffed onions to the crock pot; pour in chicken stock.

5. Cook covered on high about 4 hours.

Fruit and Nut Candied Yams

(Ready in about 4 hours | Servings 8)

Ingredients

- 2 pounds yams, peeled and thinly sliced
- 1/4 cup currants
- 1/4 cup toasted pecans, chopped
- 2/3 cup packed light brown sugar
- A pinch of salt
- 1/2 teaspoon allspice
- 1/4 teaspoon ground black pepper
- 2 tablespoons cold butter
- 1/2 cup water
- 2 tablespoons cornflour

Directions

1. Arrange yams in your crock pot, sprinkling with currants, pecans, brown sugar, salt, allspice and pepper and dotting with cold butter. Repeat the layers until you run out of ingredients.

2. Combine water and cornflour; pour into a crock pot.

3. Cover and cook on low 3 hours; then turn heat to high and cook 1 hour longer. Enjoy!

Maple Honey Ribs

(Ready in about 5 hours | Servings 6)

Ingredients
- 3 pounds pork ribs
- 1 cup canned vegetable broth
- 1/2 cup water
- 1/4 cup honey
- 3 tablespoons mustard
- 1/4 cup barbeque sauce
- 1/4 cup tamari sauce
- 1/4 cup pure maple syrup

Directions
1. In the crock, mix together all ingredients, except pork ribs.
2. Slice ribs apart; place the pork ribs in the crock pot.
3. Cover and cook 5 hours on high or until the pork falls from the bones. Serve warm with hot tomato sauce and some extra mustard, if desired.

Yam Loaf for Winter Holidays

(Ready in about 3 hours | Servings 6)

Ingredients

- 1 ¼ cups yams, peeled and coarsely grated
- 1/3 cup shallots, finely chopped
- 2 tart apples, shredded
- 1⁄4 cup golden raisins
- 1⁄8 teaspoon ground nutmeg
- 1/4 teaspoon ground cloves
- 1⁄4 teaspoon ground cinnamon
- 1⁄4 cup all-purpose flour
- 1⁄4 cup fresh orange juice
- A pinch of salt
- 1/4 teaspoon white pepper
- 1 large-sized egg

Directions

1. Mix all ingredients, except egg; adjust the seasonings to taste. Mix in egg.

2. Put the mixture into greased loaf pan; place the loaf pan on rack in your crock pot. Cover with aluminium foil.

3. Pour 2 inches hot water into the crock pot; cover and cook on high about 3 hours.

4. Let stand on wire rack at least 5 minutes; invert onto serving plates and serve.

Squash and Sweet Potato Pudding

(Ready in about 3 hours 30 minutes | Servings 6)

Ingredients

- Canola oil
- 1 cup Hubbard squash
- 1 cup carrots, sliced
- 4 medium-sized sweet potatoes, peeled and cubed
- 1/4 cup orange juice
- 2 tablespoons butter
- 1/4 cup packed light brown sugar
- 1/4 teaspoon cloves
- A pinch of salt
- 3 eggs, lightly beaten
- 1 cup miniature marshmallows

Directions

1. Oil the inside of the crock pot with canola oil.

2. Add squash, carrots, and sweet potatoes; cover and cook on high about 3 hours.

3. Remove vegetables from the crock pot; mash with remaining ingredients, except marshmallows.

4. Return mashed vegetables to the crock pot; cover and cook on high 30 minutes longer. Scatter the marshmallows on top and serve.

Rich and Creamy Potato Gratin

(Ready in about 3 hours 30 minutes | Servings 8)

Ingredients

- 2 pounds potatoes, peeled and sliced
- 1⁄4 cup green onion, sliced
- 1/2 teaspoon salt
- 1/4 teaspoon ground black pepper
- 2 tablespoons butter
- 3 tablespoons shallots, finely chopped
- 3 tablespoons all-purpose flour
- 1 cup milk
- 2 ounces reduced-fat processed cheese, cubed
- 1 cup Cheddar cheese, shredded
- 1/2 teaspoon dried basil leaves
- 1/2 teaspoon dried oregano leaves
- 1/2 teaspoon paprika

Directions

1. Layer half of the sliced potatoes and green onions in the bottom of your crock pot; sprinkle with salt and ground black pepper.

2. To make the sauce, melt butter in a small skillet; add shallots and flour and cook about 2 minutes. Gradually whisk in milk, stirring until thickened or 2 to 3 minutes.

3. Then, turn the heat to low; add remaining ingredients. Stir until everything is well combined and melted.

4. Pour half of this cheese sauce over layers in the crock pot. Repeat layers, ending with cheese sauce.

5. Cover and cook on high about 3 ½ hours. Serve warm and enjoy!

Creamy Potatoes with Smoked Ham

(Ready in about 4 hours | Servings 8)

Ingredients
- 2 pounds potatoes, sliced
- 12 ounces smoked ham, cubed
- 1 cup canned cream of mushroom soup
- 1 teaspoon dried basil leaves
- 1 cup milk
- 1 ½ cups Monterey Jack cheese
- Sea salt, to taste
- 1/4 teaspoon black pepper, freshly ground
- 1/4 teaspoon cayenne pepper
- Smoked paprika, to taste

Directions
1. Place potatoes and smoked ham in the bottom of the crock pot.
2. In a large-sized mixing bowl, combine the rest of ingredients; pour into the crock pot.
3. Cover and cook on high approximately 4 hours. Enjoy!

Creamed Root Vegetables

(Ready in about 5 hours | Servings 6)

Ingredients

- 4 small potatoes, sliced
- 1 medium-sized fennel bulb, sliced
- 1 turnips, sliced
- 1 large-sized carrot, sliced
- 2 medium parsnips, sliced
- 3 small leeks (white parts only), sliced
- 2 cloves garlic, minced
- 1/2 teaspoon dried basil leaves
- Salt, to taste
- 1/4 teaspoon ground black pepper
- 1/4 teaspoon paprika
- 1 cup chicken broth
- 1/2 cup half-and-half
- 1 cup sour cream
- 2 tablespoons cornflour

Directions

1. Combine all ingredients, except sour cream and cornflour, in your crock pot.

2. Cover and cook on high about 5 hours or until the vegetables are tender.

3. Add combined sour cream and cornflour, and continue cooking, stirring 2 to 3 minutes. Serve.

Mushroom and Zucchini Soufflé

(Ready in about 4 hours | Servings 8)

Ingredients

- 4 medium-sized eggs
- 3/4 cup whole milk
- 1/4 cup all-purpose flour
- 1 cup mushrooms, sliced
- 1 pound zucchini, chopped
- 2 tablespoons parsley, coarsely chopped
- 1 clove garlic, minced
- 1/2 teaspoon dried basil leaves
- 1/2 teaspoon dried oregano leaves
- 1/2 teaspoon dried rosemary
- 1 teaspoon salt
- 1/4 teaspoon ground black pepper
- 1/4 teaspoon cayenne pepper
- 1/2 cup Parmesan cheese, grated

Directions

1. In a mixing bowl, beat eggs, milk, and all-purpose flour until smooth.

2. Next, add remaining ingredients, except 1/4 cup Parmesan cheese.

3. Pour this mixture into casserole; sprinkle with remaining 1/4 cup of Parmesan cheese.

4. Place casserole dish on a rack in the crock pot; cover and cook 4 hours on high. Serve warm.

Cheesy Spinach and Noodle Delight

(Ready in about 4 hours | Servings 8)

Ingredients

- 1/2 cup reduced-fat cream cheese
- 1 cup cottage cheese
- 3 large eggs, lightly beaten
- 1 cup whole milk
- 1/2 cup currants
- 1/2 teaspoon allspice
- 2 cups spinach
- 1/2 cup egg noodles, cooked al dente
- 1/2 teaspoon salt
- 1/2 teaspoon ground black pepper
- 1/2 teaspoon red pepper flakes, crushed
- Parmesan cheese, as garnish

Directions

1. In a medium-sized bowl, combine cream cheese and cottage cheese; whisk eggs and add to the cheese mixture.

2. Stir in remaining ingredients, except Parmesan cheese; spoon into a soufflé dish.

3. Sprinkle with Parmesan cheese; place soufflé dish on a rack in the crock pot.

4. Cover and cook on low about 4 hours or until set.

Savory Bread Pudding

(Ready in about 5 hours | Servings 8)

Ingredients

- Non-stick cooking spray
- 8 ounces bread, cubed
- 1 teaspoon dried basil leaves
- 1/2 teaspoon mustard seeds
- 2 tablespoons butter, melted
- 1 celery rib, thinly sliced
- 1 large-sized carrots, sliced
- 8 ounces mushrooms, thinly sliced
- 1 cup shallots, finely chopped
- 1 clove garlic, minced
- 1 cup light cream
- 1 cup whole milk
- 4 eggs, lightly beaten
- 1/2 teaspoon salt
- 1/4 teaspoon ground black pepper
- 1/4 cup Provolone cheese, shredded

Directions

1. Spray bread cubes with non-stick cooking spray; sprinkle with basil and mustard seeds and toss.

2. Bake on a cookie sheet at 375 degrees F about 15 minutes or until golden brown.

3. Heat butter in a heavy skillet. Sauté celery, carrots, mushrooms, shallots and garlic about 8 minutes.

4. In a large bowl, mix the rest of ingredients, except Provolone cheese; add greased bread cubes and sautéed vegetables.

5. Spoon into greased crock pot; scatter shredded Provolone cheese on top and refrigerate overnight. Cook covered on high approximately 5 hours.

Corn and Potatoes with Shrimp

(Ready in about 2 hours | Servings 8)

Ingredients

- 4 ears corn, halved
- 2 pounds red potatoes, peeled and quartered
- 1/4 cup shrimp boil seasoning
- 1 tablespoon celery seeds
- 1 teaspoon dried basil leaves
- 4 leeks, thinly sliced
- Water, as needed
- 1 ½ pounds medium shrimp

Directions

1. Place all ingredients, except shrimp, in a crock pot.
2. Cook for 2 to 2 ½ hours on high.
3. Add the shrimp; continue to cook for 20 minutes or until the shrimp is thoroughly cooked. Serve warm.

Rich and Healthy Summer Paella

(Ready in about 6 hours | Servings 12)

Ingredients
- 1 tablespoon extra-virgin olive oil
- 2 medium-sized onions, sliced
- 3 cloves garlic, minced
- 1 pound spicy sausage
- 2 pounds tomatoes, chopped
- 2 cups chicken stock
- 2 cups clam juice
- 1 cup dry vermouth
- 2 ½ cups rice, uncooked
- 1/2 teaspoon ground cumin
- 1/2 teaspoon caraway seeds
- 1 teaspoon saffron
- Sea salt, to taste
- 1/4 teaspoon ground black pepper
- 2 tablespoons olive oil
- 1 pound fish, cubed
- 1 pound shrimp

- 1 pound fresh mussels
- 1 green pepper, minced
- 1 cup fresh green peas

Directions

1. Heat olive oil in a heavy skillet over medium heat; then, sauté the onions, garlic and sausage until sausage is browned and crumbled. Drain and transfer to the crock pot.

2. Stir in tomatoes, chicken stock, clam juice, vermouth, rice, cumin, caraway seeds, saffron, salt and black pepper; cover and cook on low for 6 hours.

3. In the same skillet, heat 2 tablespoons of oil; sauté the fish and shrimp. Transfer to the crock pot. Add remaining ingredients and cook until cooked through. Serve warm.

Rabbit in Coconut Sauce

(Ready in about 6 hours | Servings 8)

Ingredients

- 1 cup coconut milk
- 1 cup water
- 3 medium-sized tomatoes, diced
- 2 leeks, chopped
- 1 teaspoon salt
- 1 bay leaf
- 1/2 teaspoon ground black pepper
- 1/2 teaspoon red pepper flakes, crushed
- 3 pounds rabbit meat, cut into serving-sized pieces

Directions

1. In a crock pot, combine all of the ingredients.
2. Cover with a lid and heat on low for 5 to 6 hours.
3. Serve over noodles or cooked rice.

Vegetarian Potato and Eggplant Moussaka

(Ready in about 7 hours | Servings 8)

Ingredients

- 1 cup dry brown lentils, rinsed and drained
- 3 medium-sized potatoes, peeled and sliced
- 1 cup water
- 1 bouillon cube
- 1 celery rib, diced fine
- 1 medium-sized onion, sliced
- 3 cloves garlic, minced
- 1/2 teaspoon salt
- 1/4 teaspoon freshly ground black pepper
- 1/4 teaspoon ground cinnamon
- 1 teaspoon Italian seasonings
- 1 cup carrots, sliced
- 1 medium-sized eggplant, diced
- 1 cup tomatoes, diced
- 1 cup cream cheese, softened
- 2 large eggs

Directions

1. In your crock pot, layer ingredients as follows: lentils, potatoes, water, bouillon cube, celery, onions, garlic, salt, pepper, cinnamon, Italian seasonings, carrots and eggplant.

2. Cover and heat on low for 6 hours.

3. Stir in diced tomatoes, cream cheese and eggs. Cover and cook on low one more hour.

Curried Chicken Thighs with Potatoes

(Ready in about 8 hours | Servings 8)

Ingredients

- 1 tablespoon curry powder
- 1 teaspoon ground cloves
- 1 teaspoon ground nutmeg
- 1 teaspoon ground ginger
- 2 pounds chicken thighs, boneless, skinless cubed
- 1 teaspoon olive oil
- 1 medium-sized yellow onion, chopped
- 2 cloves garlic, chopped
- 1 chili pepper, minced
- 1 ½ pounds red skin potatoes, cubed
- 1 cup coconut milk

Directions

1. In a medium-sized mixing bowl, whisk the curry powder, cloves, nutmeg, and ginger. Cut the chicken thighs into bite-sized pieces. Add the chicken to the bowl; toss to coat evenly.

2. Heat olive oil in a skillet; sauté seasoned chicken pieces until they start to brown. Add to the crock pot.

3. Add the rest of the ingredients. Stir to combine. Cook approximately 8 hours on low heat setting.

Yummy Evening Pear Clafoutis

(Ready in about 3 hours | Servings 4)

Ingredients

- 2 pears, cored
- 1/2 cup rice flour
- 1/2 cup arrowroot starch
- 1 teaspoon baking soda
- 1 teaspoon baking powder
- 1/2 teaspoon xanthan gum
- A pinch of salt
- 1/4 cup sugar
- 1 teaspoon cloves
- 1/2 teaspoon grated nutmeg
- 1 teaspoon ground cinnamon
- 2 tablespoons vegetable shortening, melted
- 2 eggs
- 1 cup milk
- Maple syrup for garnish

Directions

1. Cut the pears into chunks and transfer them to the crock pot.

2. In a large-sized mixing bowl, whisk together the rice flour, arrowroot starch, baking soda, baking powder, xanthan gum, salt, sugar, cloves, nutmeg and cinnamon.

3. To make the batter, create a well in the centre of the dry ingredients; add shortening, eggs, and milk. Stir well to combine.

4. Pour batter over pear chunks in the crock pot. Vent a lid of the crock pot with a chopstick.

5. Cook on high for 3 hours. Serve with maple syrup.

Evening Risotto with Apples

(Ready in about 9 hours | Servings 6)

Ingredients

- 1/4 cup butter, melted
- 1 ½ cups Carnaroli rice
- 3 apples, peeled, cored, and sliced
- 1/4 teaspoon ground cloves
- 1 teaspoon ground cinnamon
- 1/4 teaspoon kosher salt
- 1/3 cup brown sugar
- 1 cup water
- 2 cups whole milk
- 1 cup apple juice

Directions

1. Add the butter and rice to your crock pot; stir to coat.
2. Add the rest of ingredients; stir well to combine.
3. Cover with a lid and cook on low for 9 hours. Serve warm.

Cheese and Bread Casserole

(Ready in about 3 hours | Servings 8)

Ingredients

- 1 tablespoon butter, melted
- 8 ounces Gruyère cheese, shredded
- 8 ounces cream cheese, shredded
- 8 slices bread
- 2 cups milk
- 4 eggs
- Salt, to taste
- 1/2 teaspoon dried basil
- 1/4 teaspoon paprika
- Chopped fresh chives, as garnish

Directions

1. Treat a crock pot with butter.

2. In a mixing bowl, combine the cheeses; reserve.

3. Tear the slices of bread into pieces; transfer to the crock pot. Place cheese mixture on the bread layer. Alternate layers, ending with the bread.

4. In a small-sized mixing bowl, whisk remaining ingredients, except chives. Pour over the layers in the crock pot.

5. Set the crock pot to low and cook for 3 hours. Serve garnished with fresh chives and enjoy!

French-Style Sandwiches

(Ready in about 2 hours | Servings 12)

Ingredients

- 1 cup leeks, chopped
- 1 beef bottom round roast
- 1 cup water
- 1/2 cup dry red wine
- 1 envelope au jus gravy mix
- Salt, to taste
- 1/4 teaspoon freshly ground black pepper
- 1/4 teaspoon red pepper flakes, crushed
- French bread

Directions

1. Line bottom of the crock pot with the leeks.
2. Add roast to the crock pot on top of the leeks.
3. Next, add remaining ingredients, except bread; vent a lid and cook on low for 2 hours.
4. Cut the roast into thin slices. Serve on French bread. Use the sauce for dipping.

Bratwurst and Sauerkraut Pitas

(Ready in about 2 hours 30 minutes | Servings 6)

Ingredients

- 2 tablespoons olive oil
- 2 pounds sauerkraut, drained
- 1 large-sized apple, cored and chopped
- 1 teaspoon ground cumin
- 1 teaspoon celery seeds
- 6 bratwursts
- 1/2 cup dry white wine
- 2 bay leaves
- 5-6 black peppercorns
- 1 tablespoon mustard
- 6 pita loaves

Directions

1. Heat olive oil in a heavy skillet over medium heat. Sauté the sauerkraut and apple until the sauerkraut is soft and the liquids are reduced. Add cumin and celery seeds and gently stir to combine.

2. In a separate non-stick skillet, brown the bratwurst on all sides over medium heat; drain. Pour in white wine; add bay leaves and peppercorns; cook an additional 10 minutes.

3. To make the sandwiches: roll bratwursts and sauerkraut into the pita loaves. Add mustard and wrap the sandwiches in aluminium foil. Pour water to coat the bottom of the crock pot.

4. Place the sandwiches in the crock pot. Heat on a high setting for about 2 hours.

Romantic Winter Dinner

(Ready in about 2 hours 20 minutes | Servings 6)

Ingredients

- 6 spicy sausages
- 6 long sourdough rolls
- 2 tablespoons mustard
- 2 tablespoons tomato ketchup
- 6 pickles, sliced

Directions

1. Heat a non-stick skillet over medium flame. Then, sauté the sausages until thoroughly cooked and browned; drain.

2. Next, cut off the tips of the sourdough rolls. Make sandwiches with sausage and mustard.

3. Next, wrap the sandwiches in a foil; arrange on a trivet in the crock pot. Then, you need to pour lukewarm water around the base of the trivet.

4. Cover with a lid and heat on a high setting for 2 hours. Serve with ketchup and pickles.

Kicked Up Chicken with Zucchini

(Ready in about 4 hours | Servings 6)

Ingredients

- 3 medium-sized chicken breasts, halved
- 1 cup almond milk
- 1/4 cup water
- 1/4 cup lemon juice
- 2 cloves garlic, minced
- 1 medium-sized onion, chopped
- Salt, to taste
- Red pepper, to taste
- 1 teaspoon ground ginger
- 1 teaspoon ground cumin
- 1 pound zucchini, sliced
- 1 tablespoon cornflour
- 2 tablespoons water
- 1/3 cup fresh parsley, chopped
- 4 cups rice, cooked

Directions

1. Place all ingredients, except zucchini, cornflour, water, parsley and rice, in your crock pot.

2. Cover and cook on low heat setting about 4 hours, adding zucchini during last 30 minutes of cooking time. Reserve chicken breasts.

3. Turn heat to high and continue cooking 10 minutes; stir in combined cornflour and water, stirring about 3 minutes.

4. Sprinkle with parsley; serve over rice.

Festive Cornish Hens

(Ready in about 6 hours | Servings 4)

Ingredients

- 2 frozen Cornish hens, thawed
- 1/2 teaspoon sea salt
- 1/4 teaspoon ground black pepper
- 1/2 teaspoon cayenne pepper
- 1 clove garlic, minced
- 1/3 cup chicken broth
- 2 tablespoons cornflour
- 1/4 cup water

Directions

1. Sprinkle Cornish hens with salt, black pepper and cayenne pepper; add minced garlic and place in a crock pot. Pour in chicken broth.

2. Cover and cook on low 6 hours. Remove Cornish hens and reserve.

3. Stir in combined cornflour and water, stirring 2 to 3 minutes; serve.

Salmon with Caper Sauce

(Ready in about 45 minutes | Servings 4)

Ingredients

- 1/2 cup dry white wine
- 1/2 cup water
- 1 yellow onion, thin sliced
- 1/2 teaspoon salt
- 1/4 teaspoon black pepper
- 4 salmon steaks
- 2 tablespoons butter
- 3 tablespoons flour
- 1 cup chicken broth
- 2 teaspoons lemon juice
- 3 tablespoons capers

Directions

1. Combine wine, water, onion, salt and black pepper in a crock pot; cover and cook on high 20 minutes.

2. Add salmon steaks; cover and cook on high until salmon is tender or about 20 minutes.

3. To make the sauce, in a small skillet, melt butter over medium flame. Stir in flour and cook for 1 minute.

4. Pour in chicken broth and lemon juice; whisk for 1 to 2 minutes. Add capers; serve the sauce with salmon.

Cheesy Monkfish Chowder with Cauliflower

(Ready in about 8 hours | Servings 4)

Ingredients

- 1 can (14 ounces) reduced-sodium chicken broth
- 1 pound Yukon potatoes, peeled and cubed
- 1/2 cup green onions, chopped
- 1 large-sized carrot, chopped
- 1/2 head cauliflower, broken into florets
- 1 pound monkfish, cubed
- Salt, to taste
- Crushed red pepper flakes, to taste
- 3/4 teaspoon hot pepper sauce
- 1/2 cup reduced-fat Cheddar cheese, shredded

Directions

1. Arrange first five ingredients in your crock pot. Set the crock pot to low; cook about 8 hours.

2. Next, process cooked mixture in a food processor until your desired consistency is reached; return to the crock pot.

3. Add remaining ingredients, except the hot sauce and cheese; continue cooking on low heat setting for 15 minutes longer.

4. Add the hot pepper sauce and cheese; allow to sit until Cheddar cheese is melted. Serve warm or at room temperature.

Hearty Flounder Chowder

(Ready in about 6 hours | Servings 4)

Ingredients
- 2 cups clam juice
- 3 medium-sized potatoes, cubed peeled
- 1 cup broccoli florets
- 1 cup green beans
- 1 cup leeks, chopped
- 1 carrot, chopped
- 1 rib celery, chopped
- 1 garlic clove, smashed
- 1/2 teaspoon dried marjoram leaves
- 1/4 teaspoon Mace, ground
- 1/4 teaspoon dry mustard
- 2 cups whole milk
- 8 ounces flounder fillets, skinless and cubed
- 4 ounces crabmeat
- Celery salt to taste
- 1/4 teaspoon white pepper

Directions

1. In a crock pot, place clam juice, potatoes, broccoli, green beans, leeks, carrot, celery, garlic, marjoram, mace, and dry mustard.

2. Set the crock pot to low and then cook approximately 6 hours.

3. Add milk and continue cooking for 30 minutes longer. Increase heat to high; add flounder fillets, crabmeat, celery salt and white pepper during last 15 minutes of cooking time.

4. Divide among soup bowls and serve with croutons, if desired.

Rich Seafood Soup with Bacon

(Ready in about 5 hours | Servings 4)

Ingredients

- 1 ½ cups clam juice
- 1/4 cup dry cherry wine
- 4 large-sized Yukon gold potatoes, peeled and cubed
- 1 large-sized sweet onion, chopped
- 1 rib celery, chopped
- 1 rutabaga, chopped
- 1 cup 2% reduced-fat milk
- 1 pound halibut, cubed
- A few drops of Tabasco sauce
- 3/4 teaspoon rubbed sage
- 1 teaspoon dried parsley flakes
- Salt, to taste
- Paprika to taste
- 2 slices of cooked bacon, crumbled

Directions

1. First of all, put first six ingredients into your crock pot.

2. Next, cook on high 4 to 5 hours. Replace prepared soup to a blender or a food processor; add in milk and blend until everything is well combined; return to the crock pot.

3. Add remaining ingredients, except crumbled bacon. Continue cooking an additional 15 minutes.

4. Divide the soup among four serving bowls, scatter the bacon on top and enjoy!

Refreshing Fish Chowder with Eggs

(Ready in about 8 hours | Servings 6)

Ingredients

- 2 cups water
- 1 teaspoon chicken bouillon concentrate
- 2 large-sized sweet potatoes, diced and peeled
- 1 cup baby carrot, halved
- 1/2 cup leeks, chopped
- 3/4 teaspoon dried dill weed
- 1/2 teaspoon red pepper flakes, crushed
- 2 cups 2% reduced-fat milk, divided
- 1 ½ pounds skinless fish fillets of choice, sliced
- 1 cup cucumber, seeded and chopped
- 1 tablespoon lime juice
- Celery salt to taste
- Chopped chives, as garnish
- Hard-cooked egg slices, as garnish

Directions

1. Combine first seven ingredients in your crock pot; cook on low 6 to 8 hours.

2. Add in milk during last 30 minutes. Stir in fish and cucumber during last 10 minutes of cooking time.

3. Add lime juice and celery salt and stir to combine.

4. Garnish bowls of soup with chives and hard-cooked egg slices.

Spicy Sweet Potato Chili

(Ready in about 8 hours | Servings 6)

Ingredients

- 1 pound chicken breast, boneless and skinless
- 2 cups chicken broth
- 1 tablespoon apple cider vinegar
- 2 cups canned beans, rinsed and drained
- 1 cup spring onions, chopped
- 2 cloves garlic, minced
- 1 cup button mushrooms, sliced
- 1 carrot, thinly sliced
- 2 medium-sized sweet potatoes, peeled and cubed
- 3/4 teaspoon jalapeño chilli
- 1 ½ teaspoon gingerroot
- 1 teaspoon, ground cumin
- 1/2 teaspoon ground coriander
- 1/2 teaspoon allspice
- Salt, to taste
- Ground black pepper, to taste
- Sour cream, as garnish

Directions

1. Combine all of the ingredients, except sour cream, in your crock pot.
2. Cover with a lid and cook on low heat setting 6 to 8 hours.
3. Serve with sour cream and enjoy.

Chili with Turkey and Roasted Pepper

(Ready in about 8 hours | Servings 6)

Ingredients

- 1 pound ground turkey
- 1 ½ cup canned tomatoes, stewed
- 1 can (15 ounces) red beans, rinsed drained
- 1 small-sized jalapeño pepper, minced
- 1 cup red onion, chopped
- 1/2 cup roasted red pepper, coarsely chopped
- 1/2 tablespoon chili powder
- 1/4 teaspoon ground cinnamon
- Celery salt, to taste
- Black pepper, to taste
- Smoked paprika to taste

Directions

1. Heat a non-stick skillet over medium-high flame. Brown turkey for about 5 minutes, crumbling with a fork. Transfer browned ground beef to the crock pot.

2. Add the rest of ingredients; cover with a lid and cook on low heat setting approximately 8 hours.

3. Serve with corn chips, if desired.

Black Bean Chili with Squash

(Ready in about 8 hours | Servings 6)

Ingredients

- 1 pound ground beef
- 2 cups tomato juice
- 1 cup chunky tomato sauce
- 1 cup water
- 1 tablespoon lime
- 1 ½ cups canned black beans, rinsed and drained
- 2 cups scallions, chopped
- 2 cloves garlic, minced
- 1/2 cup celery, cubed
- 2 cups butternut squash
- 1 cup zucchini
- 1 cup mushrooms
- 1 small-sized jalapeño chili, finely chopped
- 1 ½ teaspoons chili powder
- 1 sea salt
- 1/4 teaspoon ground black pepper
- 6 lime wedges

Directions

1. First of all, brown ground beef in non-stick skillet about 8 minutes, crumbling with a fork. Transfer to the crock pot.

2. Stir in remaining ingredients, except lime wedges; set the crock pot to low and cook 6 to 8 hours.

3. Serve garnished with lime wedges.

Turkey and Cannellini Bean Chili

(Ready in about 8 hours | Servings 6)

Ingredients

- 1 pound lean ground beef
- 2 cups tomato sauce
- 2 cups cannellini beans
- 1 cup spring onions, chopped
- 1 clove garlic, minced
- 1 tablespoon chili powder
- 2 teaspoons brown sugar
- 1 teaspoon celery seeds
- 1 teaspoon ground cumin
- Salt, to taste
- Ground black pepper, to taste

Directions

1. Cook ground beef in a cast-iron skillet over medium heat 8 to 10 minutes or until browned.

2. Add remaining ingredients and cook on low 6 to 8 hours.

3. Divide prepared chili among six soup bowls and serve warm with your favorite salad.

Easy Beef and Pork Chili

(Ready in about 8 hours | Servings 6)

Ingredients
- 1 tablespoon olive oil
- 1 pounds lean ground beef
- 1/2 pounds ground pork
- 2 cups pinto beans, rinsed and drained
- 2 cups stewed tomatoes
- 2 cups whole kernel corn
- 1 cup leeks, chopped
- 1/2 cup red bell pepper, chopped
- 2 tablespoons taco seasoning mix
- Salt to taste
- Black pepper to taste
- Paprika to taste
- Reduced-fat sour cream, as garnish
- Biscuits, as garnish

Directions

1. Heat the olive oil in a wide saucepan. Next, cook ground beef and pork about 10 minutes. Crumble with a fork.

2. Add the rest of ingredients, except sour cream and biscuits; cover and cook on low for about 8 hours.

3. Divide among serving bowls, serve with sour cream and biscuits.

Italian-Style Chili

(Ready in about 8 hours | Servings 8)

Ingredients

- 12 ounces lean ground turkey
- 3 cups water
- 1 can (28-ounce) tomatoes, crushed
- 1 red bell pepper, sliced
- 1 yellow bell pepper, sliced
- 1/2 cup onion, chopped
- 3 cloves garlic, minced
- 1 teaspoon ground cumin
- 2 tablespoons chili powder
- 1 dried parsley
- 2 teaspoons dried oregano leaves
- 1 teaspoon allspice
- Salt, to taste
- 1/4 teaspoon black pepper
- 1 pound spaghetti, cooked
- Reduced-fat Cheddar cheese, shredded

Directions

1. In a large non-stick skillet, brown the ground turkey over medium heat, about 5 minutes.

2. Combine turkey with remaining ingredients, except spaghetti and Cheddar cheese, in your crock pot; cook on low 8 hours.

3. Serve with spaghetti and Cheddar cheese.

Family Favourite Chili

(Ready in about 8 hours | Servings 8)

Ingredients

- 1 pound ground beef
- 1 cup onions, chopped
- 1 green bell pepper, chopped
- 1 red bell pepper, chopped
- 1 poblano pepper, minced
- 2 cloves garlic, minced
- 2 teaspoons ground cumin
- 1 teaspoon dried oregano leaves
- 1 teaspoon dried basil leaves
- 1/2 teaspoon grated ginger
- 1 tablespoon cilantro
- 2 cups tomatoes, undrained and diced
- 1 cup water
- 1 can (15 ounces) pinto beans, rinsed and drained
- 1/4 cup tomato ketchup
- 3/4 cup beer
- 1 tablespoon unsweetened cocoa

- Salt, to taste

- Black pepper, to taste

- Paprika, to taste

- Sour cream, as garnish

Directions

1. First of all, cook ground beef in lightly greased saucepan over medium heat. Cook until the beef is browned and cooked through or about 10 minutes.

2. Add beef to the crock pot. Then, add remaining ingredients, except sour cream, to the crock pot; cover with a lid and cook on low about 8 hours.

3. Garnish each bowl of chili with sour cream.

Easy Tenderloin Chili

(Ready in about 6 hours | Servings 4)

Ingredients

- 1 pound pork tenderloin, cubed
- 1 can (15-ounces) reduced-sodium fat-free vegetable broth
- 1 can (15-ounces) beans, rinsed
- 1 pound plum tomatoes, sliced
- 1 large-sized jalapeño chili, minced
- 1 tablespoon chili powder
- 1 teaspoon toasted cumin seeds
- Salt, to taste
- Black pepper, to taste
- Cayenne pepper to taste
- Corn chips, as garnish

Directions

1. Combine all ingredients, except corn chips, in a crock pot.
2. Cook covered on high about 6 hours.
3. Serve with corn chips and enjoy!

Yummy Tomato Bean Soup

(Ready in about 7 hours | Servings 6)

Ingredients

- 1 quart chicken stock
- 2 cans (15-ounce) navy beans, rinsed, drained
- 1 cup cooked bacon, chopped
- 1 pound lamb, cubed
- 1 cup scallions
- 1 rib celery, chopped
- 1 large-sized carrot, chopped
- 1 clove garlic, minced
- 1 teaspoon Italian seasoning mix
- 3 Roma tomatoes, chopped
- Salt, to taste
- Black pepper, to taste
- Cayenne pepper, to taste
- Biscuits, as garnish

Directions

1. Combine all ingredients, except biscuits, in a crock pot.

2. Next, cover and cook on low for about 7 hours.

3. Serve with biscuits and enjoy!

Lamb Chili with Ham

(Ready in about 8 hours | Servings 6)

Ingredients

- 1 quart vegetable stock
- 2 cans (15-ounce) pinto beans, rinsed, drained
- 1 cup partially cooked ham, diced
- 1 pound lamb, cubed
- 1 large-sized red onion, finely chopped
- 2 cloves garlic, minced
- 1 large-sized carrot, chopped
- 1 rib celery, chopped
- 1 teaspoon Italian seasoning mix
- 1 cup tomato sauce
- Salt, to taste
- Black pepper, to taste
- Cayenne pepper, to taste
- Sour cream, as garnish

Directions

4. Place all ingredients, except sour cream, in a crock pot.

5. Set the crock pot to low; cook your chili for 7 to 8 hours.

6. Garnish with a sour cream and serve.

Creamy Vegetable Soup

(Ready in about 4 hours | Servings 4)

Ingredients

- 2 cups vegetable stock
- 2-3 spring onions, chopped
- 3/4 cup mushrooms, thinly sliced
- 1 cup frozen artichoke hearts, thawed and finely chopped
- 1 cup light cream
- 2 tablespoons cornstarch
- Salt, to taste
- Black pepper, to taste
- Red pepper flakes, as garnish

Directions

1. Combine first four ingredients in your crock pot; cover and cook on high heat setting 4 hours.

2. Combine light cream and cornstarch. Add this mixture to the crock pot, stirring 2 to 3 minutes.

3. Season with salt and black pepper. Sprinkle each bowl of soup with red pepper flakes.

Fall Brussels sprouts Soup

(Ready in about 4 hours | Servings 4)

Ingredients

- 1 pound Brussels sprouts, halved
- 1/2 cup sweet onion, chopped
- 1 clove garlic, minced
- 1 teaspoon onion powder
- 1 teaspoon celery seeds
- 1/2 teaspoon dried rosemary leaves
- 1 cup vegetable broth
- 1 cup 2% reduced-fat milk
- Salt, to taste
- Black pepper, to taste
- Ground nutmeg, as garnish

Directions

1. Add Brussels sprouts, sweet onion, garlic, onion powder, celery seeds, rosemary, and vegetable broth to the crock pot; cover and cook on high 3 to 4 hours.

2. Pour the soup in a food processor or a blender. Add 2% reduced-fat milk. Blend until a smooth consistency is reached.

3. Season with salt and black pepper. Divide among four soup bowls and sprinkle lightly with nutmeg; serve.

Vegetarian Creamed Corn Soup

(Ready in about 4 hours 30 minutes | Servings 4)

Ingredients

- 3 ½ cups vegetable stock
- 1/2 cup scallions, chopped
- 1 large-sized carrot, chopped
- 2 medium-sized potatoes, peeled and cubed
- 1 clove garlic, minced
- 1 can (151/2 ounces) whole kernel corn, drained
- 1 cup reduced-fat milk
- 2 tablespoons cornstarch
- Celery salt, to taste
- White pepper, to taste
- Paprika, as garnish
- Sour cream, as garnish

Directions

1. Combine vegetable stock, scallions, carrot, potato, and garlic.

2. Cover and cook on high 4 hours. Purée soup in your food processor until creamy and smooth; return to the crock pot.

3. Add kernel corn and continue cooking on high 30 minutes longer. Then, add combined reduced-fat milk and cornstarch, stirring constantly 3 minutes. Sprinkle with celery salt and white pepper and stir again. Garnish with paprika and sour cream.

Rich Potato Pistou Soup

(Ready in about 4 hours 20 minutes | Servings 6)

Ingredients

- 2 quarts water
- 1 envelope onion soup mix
- 2 cups onions, chopped
- 5 cloves garlic, halved
- 4 Yukon gold potatoes, peeled and diced
- 5 plum tomatoes, seeded and chopped
- 2 medium-sized zucchini, sliced
- 3/4 teaspoon celery seeds
- 1 teaspoon dried basil leaves
- 1/4 cup Parmesan cheese, grated
- Salt, to taste
- Black pepper, to taste
- Red pepper flakes, for garnish

Directions

1. In a crock pot, combine water, onion soup mix, onions, garlic, potatoes, tomatoes, zucchini, celery seeds, and basil leaves.

2. Next, set your crock pot to high and cook 3 to 4 hours.

3. Then, add soup to a food processor. Stir in the rest of ingredients, except red pepper flakes; blend until your desired consistency is reached.

4. Return creamy soup to the crock pot; cover and cook on high 15 to 20 minutes longer; sprinkle with red pepper flakes and serve warm.

Refreshing Roasted Red Pepper Soup

(Ready in about 3 hours | Servings 4)

Ingredients

- 1 ½ cups vegetable stock
- 3/4 cup jarred roasted red peppers
- 1 tablespoon balsamic vinegar
- 1 cup water
- 1/2 cup onion, chopped
- 1 cucumber, chopped
- 1 cup potato, cubed
- 1 teaspoon ground allspice
- Salt, to taste
- White pepper, to taste
- Paprika, to taste
- 1 ½ cups plain yogurt
- 2 tablespoons cornstarch

Directions

1. In a crock pot, combine all ingredients, except yogurt and cornstarch; cover and cook on high about 3 hours.

2. Add combined yogurt and cornstarch, stirring constantly, 2 to 3 minutes.

3. Purée mixture in your food processor until smooth, creamy and uniform; set in a refrigerator and serve chilled.

Old-Fashioned Beef Stew

(Ready in about 8 hours | Servings 4)

Ingredients

- 1 cup reduced-sodium fat-free beef stock
- 1 pound beef round steak, cut into strips
- 1/2 cup dry red wine
- 2 cups green beans
- 1 onion, finely chopped
- 2 medium-sized potatoes
- 1 celery stalk, chopped
- 3 carrots, thickly sliced
- 1 teaspoon dried marjoram leaves
- 1 teaspoon dried thyme leaves
- 1 teaspoon dried sage
- Salt and black pepper, to taste
- Cayenne pepper, to taste

Directions

1. In a crock pot, combine all ingredients.
2. Cover with a lid and cook on low 8 hours.
3. Serve hot over cooked noodles.

Tangy Cucumber Soup

(Ready in about 3 hours | Servings 4)

Ingredients

- 1 ½ cups chicken stock
- 2 tablespoons apple cider vinegar
- 1 cup water
- 1/2 cup spring onions, finely chopped
- 1 cucumber, chopped
- 1 teaspoon fresh dill weed
- 1 cup potato, diced
- 1 teaspoon ground cinnamon
- Salt, to taste
- Black pepper, to taste
- Red pepper flakes, to taste
- 1 ½ cups plain yogurt
- 2 tablespoons cornstarch

Directions

1. In your crock pot, place all ingredients, except yogurt and cornstarch.

2. Cover with a lid and cook on high heat setting approximately 3 hours.

3. In a measuring cup, whisk yogurt with cornstarch; add to the crock pot and cook, stirring often, 2 to 3 minutes.

4. Pour this mixture into a food processor or a blender. Process until smooth and creamy; serve chilled.

Easy Yummy Beef Stew

(Ready in about 5 hours | Servings 6)

Ingredients

- 2 pounds beef meat, cubed
- 1 cup beef broth
- 1 sweet red bell pepper
- 1 cup scallions, chopped
- 3 cloves garlic, minced
- 1 parsnip, cubed
- 1 celery, chopped
- 1/2 cup dry red wine or beef broth
- 2 medium-sized red potato
- 2 tablespoons tomato ketchup
- 1 tablespoon apple cider vinegar
- 1/2 teaspoon dried rosemary leaves
- 2 large bay leaves
- Salt, to taste
- Black pepper, to taste
- Paprika, to taste
- 2 tablespoons cornstarch

- 1/4 cup cold water

Directions

1. Place all ingredients, except cornstarch and cold water, in your crock pot; cover and cook on high 4 to 5 hours.

2. Stir in combined cornstarch and cold water, stirring 2 to 3 minutes. Discard bay leaf and serve over rice, if desired.

Hearty Chicken Stew

(Ready in about 6 hours | Servings 4)

Ingredients

- 1 can (10 ¾ ounces) reduced-sodium condensed cream of chicken soup
- 1 ¼ cups 2% reduced-fat milk
- 1 cup water
- 1 red bell pepper, chopped
- 1 green bell pepper, chopped
- 1 poblano pepper, minced
- 1 pound chicken breasts, boneless, skinless and cubed
- 1 cup onion, sliced
- 1/2 cup turnip, diced
- 1/2 cup carrot, thinly sliced
- 1/2 teaspoon dried oregano
- 1/2 teaspoon dried rosemary
- 1/2 teaspoon celery salt
- 1/4 teaspoon red pepper flakes, crushed
- 1/4 teaspoon ground black pepper
- 2 tablespoons cornstarch

- 1/4 cup cold water

Directions

1. Combine cream of chicken soup, milk and water in a crock pot.

2. Stir in remaining ingredients, except cornstarch and water; cover and cook on low 5 to 6 hours.

3. Next, add combined cornstarch and cold water, stirring frequently 2 to 3 minutes. Serve over boiled potatoes, if desired.

Sausage and Turkey Stew

(Ready in about 5 hours | Servings 4)

Ingredients

- 2 cups smoked turkey
- 2 cups sausage links, sliced
- 1 can (28-ounce) tomatoes, diced
- 2 cloves roasted garlic, undrained
- 2 tablespoons dry vermouth
- 1 cup onion, chopped
- 1 cup whole kernel corn
- 1 bell pepper, chopped
- 1/2 teaspoon dried basil leaves
- 1/2 teaspoon dried thyme leaves
- Salt, to taste
- Black pepper, to taste
- A few drops of Tabasco sauce

Directions

1. Combine all ingredients, except Tabasco sauce, in a crock pot.
2. Cover and cook on high 5 hours.
3. Drizzle with Tabasco sauce; serve.

Turkey and Kidney Bean Stew

(Ready in about 8 hours | Servings 4)

Ingredients

- 1 pound turkey breast, cut into bite-sized pieces
- 2 cups kidney beans, rinsed and drained
- 1 can (14 ½ ounces) chicken stock
- 1 cup tomato juice
- 2 cups butternut squash, peeled and cubed
- 1 cup onion, chopped
- 1 cup sweet potato, cubed
- 1 jalapeño pepper, minced
- 1 teaspoon celery seeds, toasted
- Salt, to taste
- Black pepper, to taste
- 1/2 teaspoon dried basil
- 1/2 teaspoon dried oregano
- Fresh chives, as garnish
- 1/4 cup pine nuts, coarsely chopped

Directions

1. Put all ingredients, except fresh chives and pine nuts, into a crock pot.

2. Cover with a lid and cook on low approximately 8 hours.

3. Sprinkle each serving bowl with chives and chopped pine nuts.

Cod and Shrimp Stew

(Ready in about 4 hours | Servings 8)

Ingredients

- 1 cup clam juice
- 1 can (28-ounces) stewed tomatoes
- 1/2 cup dry white wine
- 1/2 cup onion, finely chopped
- 3 cloves garlic, minced
- 1/2 teaspoon dried thyme
- 1 teaspoon dried basil
- 1 teaspoon dried oregano leaves
- 2 bay leaves
- Salt, to taste
- Black pepper, to taste
- 1 pound cod fillets, sliced
- 1 ½ cups shrimp, peeled and deveined

Directions

1. Place all of the ingredients, except cod fillets and shrimp, in a crock pot; cover with a lid.

2. Set the crock pot to high and cook 3 to 4 hours, adding cod fillets and shrimp during last 15 minutes of cooking time. Discard bay leaves; serve with cornbread.

Summer Spiced Fish Stew

(Ready in about 5 hours 15 minutes | Servings 8)

Ingredients

- 1 cup clam juice
- 1 cup dry white wine
- 2 cans (14 ½ ounces) tomatoes, undrained and diced
- 1 cup leeks, chopped
- 1 clove garlic, minced
- 1/2 cup fennel, thinly sliced
- 1/2 head broccoli, chopped
- 1/2 celery, chopped
- 1 bay leaf
- 1/2 teaspoon dried thyme
- 3/4 teaspoon dill weed
- 1 teaspoon lemon zest, grated
- 1/4 cup parsley, chopped
- 2 tablespoon cilantro
- Salt, to taste
- Black pepper, to taste
- Cayenne pepper, to taste

- 1 pound fish fillets, cubed
- 8 ounces shrimp, peeled and deveined
- 12 mussels, scrubbed

Directions

1. Place all of the ingredients, except seafood, in a crock pot; cover and cook on high 5 hours.

2. Add fish fillets, shrimp and mussels to the crock pot and continue cooking 15 more minutes.

3. Discard bay leaf and serve warm with cooked rice.

Vegetarian Stew for All Seasons

(Ready in about 4 hours | Servings 4)

Ingredients
- 1 ½ cups vegetable stock
- 1 cup green beans
- 1 cup new potatoes
- 1/2 cup carrots, chopped
- 1/2 turnips, chopped
- 2 medium-sized plum tomatoes, chopped
- 4 green onions, sliced
- 1/2 teaspoon dried marjoram leaves
- 4 slices vegetarian bacon, fried crisp, crumbled
- 1 cup Brussels sprouts
- 10 asparagus spears, cut into small chunks
- 2 tablespoons cornstarch
- 1/4 cup cold water
- 1/4 teaspoon ground black pepper
- Salt, to taste
- 1/4 teaspoon paprika
- 3 cups cooked brown rice, warm

Directions

1. In a crock pot, arrange vegetable stock, green beans, potatoes, carrots, turnips, tomatoes, onion and marjoram leaves.

2. Cover and cook on high about 4 hours.

3. Add remaining ingredients, except cooked rice, during last 30 minutes of cooking time.

4. Serve over brown rice and enjoy!

Vegan Wheat Berry and Lentil Stew

(Ready in about 8 hours | Servings 8)

Ingredients

- 3 cups vegetable broth
- 1/2 cup dried lentils
- 1 cup wheat berries
- 1 ½ pounds potatoes, cubed
- 1 cup leeks, chopped
- 1 carrot, chopped
- 1 stalk celery, chopped
- 3 cloves garlic, minced
- Celery salt, to taste
- Black pepper, to taste

Directions

1. Put all of the ingredients into your crock pot; cover the crock pot with a lid; cook approximately 8 hours.
2. Serve with your favorite cornbread and enjoy!

Family Red Chili

(Ready in about 8 hours | Servings 4)

Ingredients

- 8 ounces ground beef sirloin
- 1 can (28-ounces) tomatoes, crushed
- 1 can (15-ounces) red kidney beans, rinsed and drained
- 1 red bell peppers, chopped
- 1 yellow bell pepper, chopped
- 1/2 cup red onion, chopped
- 1 cup large red onion
- 2 tablespoons red wine vinegar
- 1 teaspoon chili powder
- 1/4 teaspoon ground cinnamon
- 2/3 cup mild picante sauce
- Salt, to taste
- Black pepper, to taste

Directions

1. In lightly greased large skillet, brown ground beef over medium flame. Cook about 5 minutes, crumbling with a fork.

2. Transfer cooked beef to a crock pot, then, add remaining ingredients; cover and cook on low 6 to 8 hours. Serve warm with cornmeal crisps, if desired.

Turkey Chili with Kale

(Ready in about 8 hours | Servings 8)

Ingredients

- 1 tablespoon olive oil
- 1 ½ pounds lean ground turkey
- 2 cans (15-ounce) cannellini beans, rinsed and drained
- 1 cup tomato paste
- 1/2 cup red onion, chopped
- 1 bay leaf
- 1/2 teaspoon dried rosemary
- 1 teaspoon ground cumin
- 1/2 teaspoon caraway seeds
- 1 ½ cup kale, coarsely chopped
- 1/4 teaspoon black pepper
- 1/4 teaspoon cayenne pepper
- Celery salt, to taste

Directions

1. Lightly grease a large skillet with olive oil. Cook ground turkey until browned or about 10 minutes.

2. Place cooked meat and remaining ingredients, except kale, in a crock pot; cover and cook on low heat setting approximately 8 hours.

3. Add kale during the last 20 minutes of cooking time.

4. Taste, adjust the seasonings and serve warm.

Piquant Chicken Sausage Chili

(Ready in about 6 hours | Servings 4)

Ingredients

- 4 ounces chicken sausage, sliced
- 2 Roma tomatoes, chopped
- 2 heaping tablespoons tomato ketchup
- 2 cups canned beans
- 1 large-sized red onion, finely chopped
- 1 green bell pepper, chopped
- 1 red bell pepper, chopped
- 1 teaspoon ground cumin
- 1 tablespoon cilantro, chopped
- 1 tablespoon chili powder
- Salt, to taste
- Sour cream, as garnish

Directions

1. In a non-stick skillet, cook sausage until browned or about 6 minutes. Replace to the crock pot.

2. Stir in remaining ingredients, except sour cream; cover and cook on low heat setting about 6 hours.

3. Serve with a dollop of sour cream.

Pepperoni Hot Chili

(Ready in about 8 hours | Servings 8)

Ingredients

- 12 ounces turkey sausage
- 4 ounces pepperoni, sliced
- 1 can (14 1/2 ounces) diced tomatoes, undrained
- 1 ½ cup beef broth
- 1 ½ cup tomato sauce
- 1 teaspoon lemon zest
- 1 cup garbanzo beans
- 1/2 cup canned green chilies, chopped
- 1 large-sized red onion, chopped
- 1 ½ teaspoons dried Italian seasoning
- 2 tablespoons hot chili powder
- 1 tablespoon Worcestershire sauce
- Salt, to taste
- Paprika, to taste
- Hot pepper sauce, optional

Directions

1. Cook sausage and pepperoni in lightly greased saucepan over medium heat. Cook 10 to 12 minutes; transfer to a crock pot.

2. Add the rest of ingredients; cover and cook on low about 8 hours.

3. Divide among serving bowls and serve with cornbread.

Spaghetti with Beans and Asparagus

(Ready in about 3 hours | Servings 4)

Ingredients

- 1 cup vegetable stock
- 1/2 cup green beans
- 1 can (15-ounces) Great Northern beans, rinsed and drained
- 2 medium-sized tomatoes, chopped
- 2 medium-sized carrots, chopped
- 3/4 teaspoon dried rosemary leaves
- 1 pound asparagus, cut into bite-sized pieces
- 1/2 teaspoon celery salt
- 1 teaspoon onion powder
- 1 teaspoon garlic powder
- 8 ounces spaghetti, cooked
- 1/4 cup Parmesan cheese, shredded

Directions

1. In a crock pot, place vegetable stock, green beans, Great Northern beans, tomatoes, carrots, and rosemary.

2. Cook covered for 3 hours, adding asparagus pieces during last 30 minutes of cooking time.

3. Season with celery salt, onion powder and garlic powder; toss with spaghetti and Parmesan cheese. Enjoy!

Easy Spicy Green Beans

(Ready in about 4 hours | Servings 4)

Ingredients

- 1 pound green beans
- 1 can (28-ounce) petite-diced tomatoes
- 1 large-sized red onion, chopped
- 4 cloves garlic, minced
- 1 teaspoon celery seeds
- 1 teaspoon dried basil
- 1 teaspoon dried oregano
- 1 teaspoon sea salt
- 1/4 teaspoon freshly ground black pepper
- 1/4 teaspoon red pepper flakes, crushed

Directions

1. Combine all ingredients in a crock pot.

2. Cook covered on high about 4 hours or until green beans are tender.

3. Taste, adjust the seasonings and divide among serving bowls. Enjoy this easy and healthy dinner with boiled potatoes and favorite seasonal salad!

Favorite Creamy Green Beans

(Ready in about 6 hours | Servings 4)

Ingredients

- 1/2 cup sour cream
- 1/4 cup 2 % reduced-fat milk
- 1 ½ cup canned fat-free cream of mushroom soup
- 1 package (10 ounces) green beans, thawed
- 2 cloves garlic, minced
- 1 carrot, chopped
- 1 celery stalk, chopped
- Salt, to taste
- Cayenne pepper, to taste
- Chopped cashews, as garnish

Directions

1. Mix all of the ingredients, except cashews, in your crock pot.
2. Cover and cook on low heat setting about 6 hours.
3. Scatter chopped cashews on top; serve over macaroni or cooked brown rice.

Steak Roll Ups with Mushrooms

(Ready in about 6 hours | Servings 4)

Ingredients

- 1 pound beef steaks, cut into 4 serving-size portions
- 4 slices of smoked ham
- 1 cup Portobello mushrooms, chopped
- 1/4 cup dill pickle, finely chopped
- 1 large-sized sweet onion, chopped
- 1 teaspoon Dijon mustard
- 1/2 teaspoon dried tarragon
- 1 teaspoon dried basil
- 1/2 teaspoon dried oregano
- 1/2 cup beef broth
- Celery salt, to taste
- Black peppercorns, to taste
- Mayonnaise, as garnish

Directions

1. Top each portion of beef steak with ham slice.

2. In a mixing bowl, combine mushrooms, dill pickle, onion, mustard, tarragon, basil and oregano. Spread this mixture over ham.

3. Next, roll up steaks and secure them with toothpicks; place in the crock pot.

4. Pour in broth, sprinkle with celery salt and peppercorns; cook on low 5 to 6 hours. Garnish with mayonnaise and serve.

Favorite Hot Rouladen

(Ready in about 6 hours | Servings 4)

Ingredients

- 1 pound beef steaks, cut into 4 serving-size portions
- 4 slices of reduced-fat Provolone cheese
- 1 sweet red bell pepper, cut into thin strips
- 1 sweet green bell pepper, cut into thin strips
- 1/4 cup sun-dried, finely chopped
- 1 jalapeño pepper, minced
- 1/2 cup green onions, chopped
- 1 teaspoon mustard
- 1 teaspoon dried basil
- 1/2 teaspoon celery seeds
- Sea salt, to taste
- Ground black pepper, to taste
- 1/2 cup beef broth

Directions

1. Top each portion of beef steak with the slice of cheese. Then, place bell peppers on each slice of steak.

2. In a bowl, combine the rest of ingredients, except beef broth. Spread this mixture over slices of cheese.

3. Then, roll up steaks; secure with toothpicks; place in the bottom of your crock pot.

4. Pour in beef broth; cook covered on low about 6 hours. Serve warm.

Juicy Beef Short Ribs

(Ready in about 8 hours | Servings 4)

Ingredients

- 1/2 cup dry red wine
- 1/2 cup beef broth
- 1 teaspoon mustard
- 4 large-sized carrots, sliced
- 1 large-sized red onion, cut into wedges
- 1 heaping tablespoon cilantro
- 1/2 teaspoon dried tarragon
- 2 pounds beef short ribs

Directions

1. Arrange all ingredients in a crock pot, placing beef short ribs on the top.
2. Cover and cook on low approximately 8 hours.
3. Serve warm with some extra mustard.

Easy Italian-Style Meatloaf

(Ready in about 7 hours | Servings 4)

Ingredients

- 1 ½ pounds lean ground beef
- 1 cup quick-cooking oats
- 1 teaspoon lemon zest
- 1/2 cup milk
- 1 medium-sized egg
- 1/4 cup tomato catsup
- 1/2 cup scallions, chopped
- 1 green bell pepper, chopped
- 1 teaspoon granulated garlic
- 1 teaspoon Italian seasoning
- 1 teaspoon sea salt
- 1/2 teaspoon ground black pepper

Directions

1. Mix all ingredients until everything is well incorporated; place your meatloaf on slow cooker liner in a crock pot.

2. Cover and cook on low 6 to 7 hours.

3. Serve over mashed potatoes and enjoy!

Cheesy Everyday Meatloaf

(Ready in about 6 hours | Servings 4)

Ingredients
- 1/2 pound lean ground pork
- 1/2 pound lean ground beef
- 1/2 cup reduced-fat cream cheese
- 1 cup quick-cooking oats
- 2 tablespoons Worcestershire sauce
- 1 medium-sized egg
- 1/4 cup tomato ketchup
- 1/2 cup onion, chopped
- 1 green bell pepper, chopped
- 1/2 teaspoon ground ginger
- 1 clove garlic, minced
- 1 teaspoon sea salt
- 1/2 teaspoon ground black pepper
- 1/2 cup reduced-fat Cheddar cheese, grated

Directions

1. In a large-sized mixing bowl, combine all of the ingredients, except Cheddar cheese. Shape into a meatloaf.

2. Place the meatloaf on slow cooker liner in a crock pot.

3. Cook on low approximately 6 hours.

4. Scatter grated Cheddar cheese on top and let stand until cheese is melted. Serve.

Curried Peanut Meat Loaf

(Ready in about 6 hours | Servings 4)

Ingredients

- 1 cup quick-cooking oats
- 1 teaspoon grated ginger
- 1/2 cup milk
- 1 egg
- 1/4 cup chutney, chopped
- 1/2 cup onion, chopped
- 1 sweet red bell pepper, chopped
- 1 teaspoon granulated garlic
- 1 teaspoon dried basil
- 1/3 cup chopped peanuts
- 1 teaspoon curry powder
- 1 teaspoon sea salt
- 1/2 teaspoon ground black pepper
- 1 ½ pounds ground beef and pork, mixed

Directions

1. Line a crock pot with a wide strip of aluminium foil.

2. In a large mixing bowl, combine oats, ginger, milk, egg, chutney, onion, bell pepper, garlic, basil, peanuts, curry powder, sea salt and black pepper. Mix well to combine.

3. Stir in ground meat and mix again. Shape the mixture into a round loaf.

4. Place in the crock pot; set crock pot to low and cook 6 hours. Serve warm or at room temperature.

Mom's Spiced Mashed Beans

(Ready in about 8 hours | Servings 10)

Ingredients

- 9 cups water
- 3 cups canned pinto beans, rinsed
- 1 yellow onion, cut into wedges
- 1/2 poblano pepper, seeded and minced
- 2 cloves garlic, minced
- 1 tablespoon Cajun seasoning
- 1 teaspoon fine sea salt
- 1 teaspoon ground black pepper
- 1 teaspoon cayenne pepper

Directions

1. Arrange all of the ingredients in a crock pot.
2. Cook on high heat setting for 8 hours.
3. Strain and reserve the liquid. Mash the beans, adding the reserved liquid as needed. Serve with sausage and your favourite salad.

Kicked Up Cajun Jambalaya

(Ready in about 8 hours | Servings 12)

Ingredients

- 1 (28-ounce) can tomatoes, diced
- 1 pound chicken breast, skinless, boneless and cut into bite-sized pieces
- 1 pound Andouille sausage, sliced
- 1 large-sized onion, chopped
- 1 celery stalk, chopped
- 1 bell pepper, chopped
- 1 cup chopped celery
- 1 cup chicken stock
- 1 teaspoon dried basil leaves
- 1 teaspoon dried oregano
- 1 teaspoon Cajun seasoning
- 1 teaspoon cayenne pepper
- 1 pound frozen cooked shrimp without tails
- 1 cup cooked rice

Directions

1. In a crock pot, place all of the ingredients, except shrimp and cooked rice.

2. Cover and cook 8 hours on low.

3. Stir in the shrimp and cooked rice during the last 30 minutes of cooking time. Enjoy!

Tangy Pork Roast

(Ready in about 8 hours | Servings 8)

Ingredients
- 1 large red onion, sliced
- 2 cloves garlic, minced
- 2 pounds pork loin roast, boneless
- 1 cup water
- 2 tablespoons brown sugar
- 3 tablespoons dry red wine
- 2 tablespoons Worcestershire sauce
- 1/4 cup tomato juice
- 1/2 teaspoon salt
- 1/2 teaspoon black pepper

Directions

1. Arrange the slices of onion and minced garlic over the bottom of a crock pot; place the roast on top.

2. In a measuring cup or a mixing bowl, mix together the rest of ingredients; pour over pork loin roast.

3. Cover and cook on high for 3 to 4 hours or on low for 8 hours. Serve over mashed potatoes.

Hearty Stuffed Cabbage Leaves

(Ready in about 8 hours | Servings 4)

Ingredients

- 8 large-sized cabbage leaves
- 1 pound lean ground beef
- 1/4 cup onion, finely chopped
- 1/4 cup water
- 1 red bell pepper
- 1/4 cup cooked rice
- 3/4 teaspoon salt
- 1/4 teaspoon ground black pepper
- 1 ½ cup tomato sauce
- 1 can (16-ounce) tomatoes, diced

Directions

1. Place cabbage leaves in boiling water and cook until softened; drain.

2. Combine together ground beef and remaining ingredients, except tomato sauce and tomatoes. Stuff cabbage leaves, folding ends and sides over.

3. Stir in tomato sauce and tomatoes; cover and cook on low approximately 8 hours.

4. Serve with a dollop of sour cream.

Milk Braised Pork Loin

(Ready in about 4 hours | Servings 8)

Ingredients

- Ground black pepper, to taste
- Fine cooking salt, to taste
- 1 pork loin roast, boneless
- 1 cup green onions, chopped
- 2 cloves garlic, minced
- 1/2 cup milk
- 1/4 cup dry red wine
- 1 teaspoon dried sage
- 1 teaspoon dried rosemary
- Chives for garnish

Directions

1. Rub black pepper and salt into pork loin roast. Place in a crock pot.

2. Scatter chopped onions and minced garlic on top; then add combined milk and wine. Sprinkle with sage and rosemary.

3. Cover and cook on low about 4 hours.

4. Sprinkle with fresh chives and serve!

Mashed Potatoes with Carrots

(Ready in about 3 hours | Servings 8)

Ingredients

- 5 pounds red potatoes, cut into chunks
- 2 cloves garlic, minced
- 2 carrots, thinly sliced
- 1 cube chicken bouillon
- 1 cup sour cream
- 1 cup cream cheese
- 1/2 cup butter
- 1/2 teaspoon salt
- 1/2 teaspoon ground black pepper

Directions

1. In a large stockpot of boiling water, cook the potatoes, garlic, carrots and chicken bouillon about 15 minutes. Reserve water.

2. Next, mash boiled potatoes with sour cream and cream cheese.

3. Transfer the mashed potato to the crock pot; cover the crock pot with a lid, cook on low for about 3 hours.

4. Stir in butter; sprinkle with salt and black pepper; serve.

Holiday Cooked Ham

(Ready in about 8 hours | Servings 24)

Ingredients

- 1 cured, bone-in picnic ham
- 2 cups packed brown sugar
- 1/4 teaspoon ground cloves
- 2 tablespoons balsamic vinegar

Directions

1. Spread brown sugar and ground cloves on the bottom of the crock pot.
2. Place the ham in the crock pot and then add balsamic vinegar.
3. Cover and cook on low approximately 8 hours.

Family Favourite Apple Butter

(Ready in about 10 hours | Servings 24)

Ingredients

- 5 pounds apples, peeled, cored and chopped
- 4 cups brown sugar
- 1/2 teaspoon grated nutmeg
- 1 tablespoon ground cinnamon
- 1/2 teaspoon ground cloves
- A pinch of salt

Directions

1. Place the chopped apples in your crock pot.

2. In a medium-sized bowl, mix remaining ingredients until everything is well combined.

3. Pour this mixture over the apples in the crock pot and stir to combine.

4. Cover and cook on high for 1 hour. Turn heat to low and then cook about 9 hours. Stir with a whisk and refrigerate.

Italian-style Chicken with Broccoli

(Ready in about 9 hours | Servings 6)

Ingredients

- 3 chicken breasts, skinless and boneless
- 1 cup Italian-style salad dressing
- 1 ½ cups cream of chicken soup
- 1 cup chicken stock
- 1 cup cream cheese
- 1 teaspoon dried oregano
- 1/2 teaspoon dried basil
- Celery salt, to taste
- Ground black pepper, to taste
- Cayenne pepper, to taste

Directions

1. In a crock pot, combine the chicken breasts with Italian-style dressing.

2. Cover, set the crock pot to low and cook for 8 hours.

3. Shred the chicken meat and return to the crock pot. In a medium-sized mixing bowl, mix remaining ingredients.

4. Pour over the shredded chicken in the crock pot; add broccoli. Turn the heat to low and continue cooking for about 1 hour.

Herbed Salmon Loaf with Sauce

(Ready in about 5 hours | Servings 4)

Ingredients

For the Salmon Meatloaf:
- 1 cup fresh bread crumbs
- 1 can (7 ½ ounce) salmon, drained
- 1/4 cup scallions, chopped
- 1/3 cup whole milk
- 1 egg
- 1 tablespoon fresh lemon juice
- 1 teaspoon dried rosemary
- 1 teaspoon ground coriander
- 1/2 teaspoon fenugreek
- 1 teaspoon mustard seed
- 1/2 teaspoon salt
- 1/4 teaspoon white pepper

For the Sauce:
- 1/2 cup cucumber, chopped
- 1/2 cup reduced-fat plain yogurt
- 1/2 teaspoon dill weed

- Salt, to taste

Directions

1. Line your crock pot with a foil.

2. Mix all ingredients for the salmon meatloaf until everything is well incorporated; form into loaf and place in the crock pot.

3. Cover with a suitable lid and cook on low heat setting 5 hours.

4. Combine all of the ingredients for the sauce; whisk to combine.

5. Serve your meatloaf with prepared sauce.

Lazy Man Mac and Cheese

(Ready in about 4 hours | Servings 4)

Ingredients

- Non-stick cooking spray-butter flavour
- 16 ounces macaroni of choice
- 1/2 cup butter, melted
- 1 (12-ounce) can evaporated milk
- 1 cup milk
- 4 cups Colby jack cheese, grated

Directions

1. Lightly grease a crock pot with cooking spray.

2. First of all, cook your favourite macaroni according to package directions; rinse and drain; transfer to the crock pot.

3. Add the rest of ingredients and stir well. Cook on low heat setting 3 to 4 hours. Enjoy!

Mediterranean Chicken with Zucchini

(Ready in about 8 hours | Servings 4)

Ingredients

- 4 medium-sized chicken breasts, skinless
- 2 cups petite-diced tomatoes
- 1 stock cube
- 1/2 cup dry white wine
- 1/2 cup water
- 1 medium zucchini, sliced
- 1 large-sized onion, chopped
- 1/3 cup fennel bulb, chopped
- 1 teaspoon ground cumin
- 1 teaspoon dried basil leaves
- 1 bay leaf
- A pinch of black pepper
- 1/4 cup olives, pitted and sliced
- 1 teaspoon lemon juice
- 3 cups cooked rice

Directions

1. Place all ingredients, except olives, lemon juice and cooked rice, in a crock pot; cover and cook on low about 8 hours, adding pitted olives during last 30 minutes of cooking time.

2. Add lemon juice; discard bay leaf. Serve over cooked rice and enjoy.

Mediterranean Stuffed Spaghetti Squash

(Ready in about 8 hours | Servings 4)

Ingredients

- 1 medium-sized spaghetti squash, halved lengthwise and seeded
- 2 Roma tomatoes, diced
- 2 cans (6-ounces) tuna in water, drained and flaked
- 1 teaspoon dried basil leaves
- 1 teaspoon dried oregano leaves
- 1/2 teaspoon dried thyme
- Salt, to taste
- Black pepper, to taste
- Cayenne pepper, to taste
- 1/2 cup water
- 1/4 cup Pecorino Romano, grated

Directions

1. Place squash halves on a plate.

2. In a measuring cup or a mixing bowl, combine all of the ingredients, except water and Pecorino Romano. Spoon this mixture into squash halves and place in the crock pot.

3. Add water to the crock pot; cover and cook 6 to 8 hours on low.

4. Sprinkle with Pecorino Romano and serve.

www.ingramcontent.com/pod-product-compliance
Lightning Source LLC
Chambersburg PA
CBHW071819080526
44589CB00012B/850